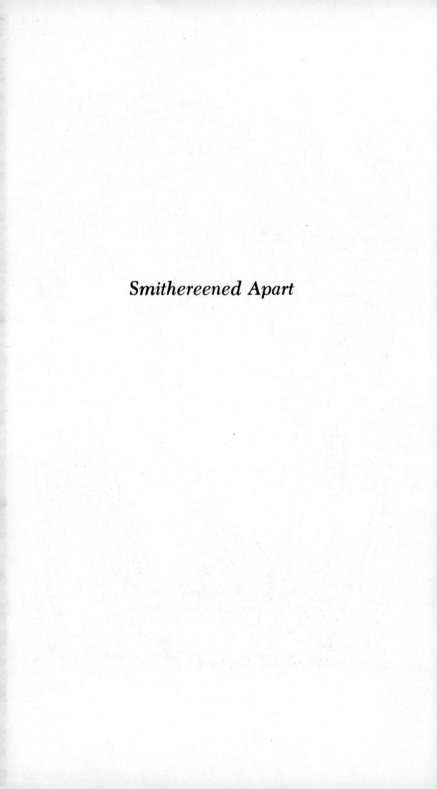

Smithereened Apart

Drawing by John Johns

HART CRANE, 1929

SMITHEREENED APART:
A Critique of Hart Crane

BY

SAMUEL HAZO

Ohio University Press

Athens, Ohio

Acknowledgment is made for permission to quote from *Modern Poetry* by Hart Crane, reprinted by permission of Coward-McCann, Inc., from *Revolt in the Arts* by Oliver Sayler. Copyright © 1929, 1957 by Oliver Sayler.

To Liveright Publishing Corporation appreciation is expressed for permission to quote from *The Collected Poems of Hart Crane*, copyright © R–1961, Liveright Publishing Corp.

Permission from the publisher to reprint from the following is gratefully acknowledged: *Hart Crane's Sanskrit Charge* by L. S. Dembo, Cornell University Press; *The Heel of Elohim* by Hyatt Waggoner, University of Oklahoma Press; *Letters on Some Modern Poets* by Margaret F. LeClair, Carnegie Press; *Hart Crane* by Philip Horton, The Viking Press; *Exile's Return: A Literary Odyssey of the 1920's* by Malcolm Cowley, The Viking Press; "The Structure of Hart Crane's *The Bridge*" by Bernice Slote, *The University of Kansas City Review;* "Fish Food: An Obituary to Hart Crane" by John Wheelright from *Selected Poems,* copyright 1941 by New Directions, reprinted by permission of New Direction Publishers; and to Brom Weber for permission to use the photographs in his book *Hart Crane* as a basis for the drawings herein reproduced.

This book was originally printed by Barnes and Noble, Inc. in 1963 as No. 7 in the American Authors and Critics Series under the title, *Hart Crane: An Introduction and Interpretation.*

PREFACE

When this study appeared in 1963, it was the first book-length treatment of Hart Crane and his work. Since then, as the updated bibliography in this book substantiates, there have been many other books that have been published by various hands as interest in the poetry of Crane has increased. Today, in addition to these books, there are innumerable articles, monographs and even a recently created Hart Crane Newsletter to provide critical and biographical information to this growing readership.

After having evaluated my study against and beside the corpus of other material that has been written since 1963, I have concluded that my various interpretations and commentaries still seem to me as valid as I thought they were when I first wrote them. In fact, I have observed that the critical assumptions that motivated my critique of Crane's poems are quite similar to those in later works by R. W. B. Lewis, Herbert Leibowitz, Sherman Paul and various others. It, therefore, confirms me in my conviction that my disinclination to accept the critical fiats of Yvor Winters, Alan Tate and critics of their persuasion was an instinct that other critics of the sixties and seventies came to share, if not consequentially, then, at least, in subsequence. By now it is commonly agreed that Crane was not the Pindaric failure that previous critics believed him to be but really, along with e. e. cummings, was one of the genuine romantic poets of the early half of the twentieth century.

The re-issue of this book, which went out of print in its original and second edition in the late sixties, is especially gratifying to me since it creates an opportunity to introduce it to a new generation of students and to re-introduce it to the small but growing shelf of Crane studies to date. The supplement to the bibliography should make the book current to those whose interests are primarily bibliographical, but the book's critical thrust seems to me as viable now as it was more than ten years ago. For this reason I have changed nothing in the original edition except the book title, which is derived directly from Crane's "The Hurricane." For making this re-issue possible, I am grateful to Patricia Fitch of the Ohio University Press. Thanks are also due to Ernest Stefanik for invaluable bibliographical assistance.

S. H.

CONTENTS

CHRONOLOGY

1899   Harold Hart Crane born July 21, in Garretsville, Ohio, the only son of Clarence Arthur and Grace Hart Crane.

1909   Sent to live at the home of his maternal grandmother in Cleveland following a quarrel between his parents.

1913   Enrolled at East High School in Cleveland and began to write verse.

1915   Journey with his mother to his grandmother's plantation on the Isle of Pines in the West Indies. Returned to Cleveland where he met Mrs. William Vaughn Moody, the widow of the poet, who encouraged his interest in poetry.

1916   First poem "C33" published in *Bruno's Weekly*. Toured the West with his mother. After his parents' final separation and divorce, departed for New York.

1917   Under the guardianship of Carl Schmitt, a friend of the family, widened his circle of friends (writers Alfred Kreymborg and Maxwell Bodenheim) and quickened his poetic interests. Began work on a popular novel, but soon gave it up. Completed "The Bathers."

1918   Became associate editor of *The Pagan*. Returned to Cleveland and tried, in vain, to enlist for military service. After the war, employed as a reporter for the Cleveland newspaper *Plain Dealer*.

1919   Became manager of the advertising department of *The Little Review*. Resigned his position and found employment with Rheinthal and Newman Agency. In November, accepted a clerkship in one of his father's candy stores in Akron, Ohio.

1920   Worked in father's business in Cleveland. Canvassed the area around Washington, D.C. for candy company franchises.

1921   Severed all ties with his father and took up residence in Cleveland in order to resume his apprenticeship to poetry with full dedication. Completed "Black Tambourine."

1922   Wrote advertising copy for Corday & Gross in Cleveland. Friendships with William Sommer and Ernest Nelson (both painter-lithographers) sustained his literary interests but had no salutary effect upon his homosexuality and increasing alcoholism.

1923 Returned to New York in March to live temporarily with Gorham Munson (author, editor, and critic) and wife at 4 Grove Street in Greenwich Village. Wrote "Praise for an Urn." With the help of Waldo Frank (novelist and critic) took a job with the J. Walter Thompson Advertising Company.

1924 Found new advertising employ with Sweets Catalogue Service and moved into a room once occupied by Roebling, the Brooklyn Bridge architect, at 110 Columbia Heights. Began work on "Voyages."

1925 Received an advance of $1,000 from Otto Kahn (New York banker and patron of artists) enabling Crane to continue work on *The Bridge*. Shared a home in Patterson, New York, with Allen Tate (the poet) and wife Caroline.

1926 Traveled with Waldo Frank to the Isle of Pines, remaining there to work on *The Bridge* until a hurricane wrecked the plantation home and forced him to return to New York. *White Buildings,* his first book of poems, published by Liveright in December.

1927 Moved to Paterson, New Jersey, and began "The River."

1928 Served as traveling secretary to Herbert Wise, stockbroker, on a trip to California. In December, sailed for Europe, with the intention of settling on Majorca, off the coast of Spain, and finishing *The Bridge*.

1929 Bogged down in assorted debaucheries in Paris and returned to New York in July.

1930 Liveright edition of *The Bridge*, published in April, three months after a limited edition (the Black Sun edition) was printed in Paris. Employed briefly as a writer for *Fortune* magazine. Awarded a Guggenheim Fellowship and sailed for Mexico, resolving to write an epic on the conquest of Mexico.

1931 Settled in Mixcoac, became part of an artists' colony which included writer Katherine Anne Porter and painter David Alfaro Siqueiros, and lived with Peggy Baird, former wife of the writer Malcolm Cowley.

1932 On his return to the United States to settle his father's estate, ended his life by leaping from the stern of the S.S. "Orizaba" into the sea.

It is to be learned—
This cleaving and this burning,
But only by the one who
Spends out himself again.

—*"Legend"*

I know that I run the risk of much criticism by defending such theories as I have, but as it is part of a poet's business to risk not only criticism—but folly—in the conquest of consciousness I can only say that I attach no intrinsic value to what means I use beyond their practical service in giving form to the living stuff of the imagination.

—*General Aims and Theories*

⋖§ INTRODUCTION

THE GENERATION of writers to which Hart Crane belonged grew up in the 1920's in a curious "mid-kingdom." Confronted as they were in the unsettled period after the First World War by an outdated Victorian morality wedded to an amoral world of burgeoning American business, these writers came to maturity in a society they had already outgrown. They had to find their way through the woods, and it was not altogether surprising that many of them momentarily or permanently lost their direction. A good number of Crane's contemporaries chose the path of least resistance. They were the ones who created what has remained the stereotyped impression of the "twenties"—an image of the flapper superimposed upon the shallow and crumbling world of F. Scott Fitzgerald's Gatsby. Yet, there were a few who chose another road. Riled by the dehumanizing values of H. L. Mencken's *boobus americanus,* these young men and women accepted the challenge of forging for themselves a place in a society that had not only excluded them but was also indifferent to them. From this group emerged the essayists, novelists, and poets who would create the abiding literature of those nameless years.

The problems challenging the writers of the twenties were awesome. Not the least of their troubles was that they were uniquely unsuited to Main Street. The petite bourgeoisie tended to regard the serious writer as one who simply did not "belong," who did not pay the expected obeisance to the accepted values of the time.

I

Indeed, if the writer did not openly attack these values, he seemed determined to ridicule them, as Mencken did, or satirize them, as Sinclair Lewis did.

It was for this reason that many artists and writers began to look elsewhere for a place where they belonged. Magnetized by the Bohemian activity in New York and Paris, they migrated to these centers in search of kindred spirits, guidance, and audiences. Crane himself lived in Greenwich Village and on the Left Bank during the twenties, and there were others: John Dos Passos, Malcolm Cowley, Ezra Pound, Sherwood Anderson, Ernest Hemingway, T. S. Eliot, E. E. Cummings, Eugene O'Neill, and Edna St. Vincent Millay, to name only a few. But the real challenge confronting Crane and his contemporaries was more than a geographic one. Their problems as writers could not be solved by a mere change of address from the cities and towns of Ohio, Michigan, Illinois, and Massachusetts to the more amenable locations of New York and Paris. The braver artists soon came to realize that bitterness and escape could bring no permanent solutions. Changes of address were only prefaces to more demanding spiritual encounters. Their first challenge, therefore, was to find a way to keep their contempt for America's postwar cultural ideals from poisoning their art and the genuine love that many of them had for their country. At the same time there were the continual demands of realizing and perfecting their styles, seeking the elusive synthesis of vision in their art, and achieving the uneasy reconciliation of art and prudence.

But there were still other problems awaiting solution, and solutions came, if at all, only after an agony of effort, thought, and sacrifice. If one rejected the world of Babbitt, upon what standards of value, implied or stated, was one basing such a rejection? What did one have to offer that was better? Was the ultimate solution to the dilemma of the American writer the solution of voluntary exile? Was it possible to effect a peace between man and the dynamo? If one could not "go home again," where else was there to go and what should one be seeking? Was it necessary to return to Whitman to find the real roots of a literature that would be truly American? Could the dilemmas be resolved by seeking help from the Guggenheim Foundation, by starting a new magazine, or by taking a job in an advertising agency and writing "on the side"?

It was to the credit of many young writers of the twenties that they could find answers to their problems, for they went on to cre-

ate a literature which Americans still look back on with pride.
Hart Crane also solved his problems as an artist in such moving
and powerful monuments of poetic creations as "Praise for an
Urn," "Chaplinesque," "The Wine Menagerie," and "Voyages"
from *White Buildings*, and "Ave Maria," "The Dance," "National
Winter Garden," and "Atlantis" from *The Bridge*. But these answers sustained him for a brief time only. Had he been as successful in solving his personal problems, he might have faced the future with more wisdom, confidence, and hope. Unfortunately, he
gave himself no second chance.

~§ THE LIFE

HAROLD HART CRANE was born in Garrettsville, Ohio, on July 21, 1899, the only child of Clarence Arthur and Grace Hart Crane, whose lives were to become more and more incompatible until their divorce in 1916. Almost from the day of his birth the boy was fated to be the emotional victim of two inescapable pressures. The first was his father's ambition to have his son continue his own dream of success in the candy business. The other was the scapegoat role he was forced to assume when alone with his mother. Often he simply became his mother's whipping boy and bore the abuse of her spells of depression, induced by her husband's abuse, possessiveness, or deliberate absence. Both of these pressures became progressively more intense in their effect on the young Crane, and it would be difficult to deny that much of his instability of personality and insecurity as an adult was derivative in large part from the titanic conflicts between his mother and father.

Because the elder Crane was more interested in an heir than in a son inclined to poetry, the growing boy naturally turned toward his mother. At times he found her amenable to his questions; but more often she would direct toward him, rather than toward her husband, her anger and humiliation. The sense of divided loyalty, insecurity and unnecessary grief that his parents' selfishness was to have upon Crane can only be imagined. Years later, though,

he would write his mother about his early lack of parental understanding and familial security:

> I don't want to fling accusations, etc., at anybody, but I think it's
> time you realized that for the last eight years my youth has been a
> rather bloody battleground for yours and father's sex life and
> troubles. With a smoother current around me I would now be well
> along in some college taking probably some course of study which
> would enable me upon leaving to light upon, far more readily than
> otherwise, some decent form of employment.

When the parental quarrels threatened to break up the family
entirely, Crane was sent to live at the home of his maternal grandmother in Cleveland. Here Hart stayed until 1916, except for a
brief voyage in 1915 with his mother to his grandmother's plantation on the Isle of Pines in the West Indies; and here in Cleveland
he also felt the deeper and irresistible pull toward poetry as his
vocation. This was confirmed in him and further strengthened
when his father, not altogether unsympathetic toward poets, introduced him to the widow of William Vaughn Moody, the poet.
Mrs. Moody immediately appreciated the boy's talents and encouraged his poetic development.

In the fall of 1916, the combative parents, who had become
temporarily reconciled and had come to live in Cleveland, resumed
their quarrel. This time their separation became final and ended
in divorce. Hart no longer had any reason to stay in Cleveland
and so departed for New York in search of a sounding board for
his newly developing poetic interests.

New York in the winter of 1916–17 was a city of excitement
and enthusiasm, a clearing house for idealists, volunteers, and
armed forces personnel; for Crane, the city was a place of inspiration. The Great War had stirred up the people and had had its
effect as well on the literary forces: the young circles around
Poetry, The Little Review, The Pagan, and *The Seven Arts.*
Neophytes and critics gathered to discuss Edgar Lee Masters'
Spoon River Anthology, Robert Frost's *North of Boston,* and the
poems of Carl Sandburg, Amy Lowell, Ezra Pound, John Gould
Fletcher, and Vachel Lindsay.

Supported for a time by a forbearing artist named Carl Schmitt,
a friend of the Crane family, Crane eagerly steeped himself in the
invigorating atmosphere which had been so alien to his life in
Ohio. His mother soon came to live with him and encouraged him
to prepare for college in the fall. Despite an initial interest in this
project, he lacked the self-discipline to continue and turned instead

to reading his favorite books and magazines and indulging in a newly found social life. After his mother returned to Cleveland, Crane began what he thought would be a popular novel; but his needs soon turned his hand to short-story writing for immediate profit. In the meantime he continued to absorb the education of New York.

In 1918 he returned to Cleveland at his mother's request. His efforts to volunteer in the draft for military service came to naught, and after the Armistice he was uncertain about returning to New York. When he did go back, it was only to a job which quickly disappointed him. Finally, in October, 1919, he made a decision which he had for some time avoided: to accept his father's offer of a clerkship in the candy company in Akron. He hoped somehow, while working there, to be able to perfect his art and simultaneously to continue his extensive studies in William Butler Yeats, Ezra Pound, the Elizabethan dramatists, Walt Whitman, William Blake, and the French Symbolists.

Once in Akron, however, Crane was to discover the impossibility of reconciling his ambitions as a poet with the materialistic world of his father. He had neither the time nor strength to maintain citizenship in two worlds. His work soon took Hart to his father's factory in Cleveland, where he was equally unsatisfied, and eventually he succumbed to the suggestion to canvass the Washington, D.C. area for possible franchises for the Crane Candy Company. While his failure in this project also discouraged him greatly, he did hang on a bit longer to the hope of supporting himself by working in his father's company. Inevitably father and son quarreled, and Hart left his father's employ finally in April, 1921.

After almost a year of relative unemployment, Crane began anew the attempt to support himself—by writing advertising copy in Cleveland. Fortified for a time by a sense of financial independence and secure in his friendships with two painter-lithographers, William Sommer and Ernest Nelson, Crane devoted his evenings to the craft and study of poetry. Eventually, however, this arrangement proved unsatisfactory. In his biography of Crane, Brom Weber has written that in this period Crane was "unable to foresee that in fashioning advertising slogans and paragraphs he would of necessity be weakening his integrity as a writer, as well as sapping his creative energies." [1] But if his Cleveland employ-

---

[1] *Hart Crane: A Biographical and Critical Study* (New York: The Bodley Press, 1948).

ment proved abortive, it was not because Crane was not trying to come to terms with the problem of discovering his place in the world. Had it not been for his limited education, he might have found work that would have created less conflict between his poetic interests and his social activities. Unfortunately, only a few possibilities were open to him, and these, like the clerkship in Akron and the canvasser's job in Washington, were so unsuited to Crane's temperament that each led to a similarly frustrating end.

～§ §～

While Crane lived in Akron and in Cleveland two strains in his character began to manifest themselves, and each was to be a part of his personality until his death. The first was his commitment to poetry, which was strengthened after he broke with his father. By severing those ties he was able to preserve the integrity he would otherwise have lost. Even though his problems of earning a living were to be compounded by this decision, he was able thereafter to devote himself more singlemindedly to the pursuit of his art, and his devotion to poetry soon began to bear fruit. He completed "Black Tambourine" in 1921, "Chaplinesque" in 1922, and "Praise for an Urn" in 1923—poems which marked the beginning of a lyrical moment that would culminate in the publication of Crane's first book of poems, *White Buildings,* in 1926.

The second strain was Crane's sexual deviation. From the time he first revealed a homosexual proclivity to Gorham Munson, who was the editor of *The Pagan* and Crane's close friend in New York, Crane was never able to free himself from this perversion. One can only imagine Munson's dismay when he read Crane's candid letter of December, 1919, from Akron:

> So many things have happened lately with the rush of Christmas, etc., that I am tired out and very much depressed today. This "affair" that I have been having has been the most intense and satisfactory one of my whole life, and I am all broken up at the thought of leaving him. Yes, the last word will jolt you.

As time passed, Crane came to discuss the question of homosexuality openly with friends or total strangers. Eventually he told his own mother. It was his custom to document the acceptability of homosexual behavior by citing the lives of Whitman, Leonardo, and others. How much his knowledge of Plato figured into these justifications can only be surmised, but Crane read Plato from his youth and certainly must have known of Plato's

7

tolerence of homosexuality. Crane's biographer, Philip Horton, has attempted with admirable tact and restraint to analyze the causes of Crane's homosexuality in terms of his abnormal childhood as well as his aesthetic temperament. Assuredly, the lack of familial security which contributed to Crane's instability had much to do with this inclination. Regardless of the cause, the fact remains that Crane's homosexual relations became progressively more frequent and compulsive during his twenties. This vice, together with his alcoholism and the beatings he periodically received in saloons or during his postmidnight solicitations, tended not only to weaken but to age him. Yvor Winters mentions in an essay that he saw Crane in 1927 when he "was approximately 29 years old; his hair was graying, his skin had the dull red color with reticulated grayish traceries which so often goes with advanced alcoholism, and his ears and knuckles were beginning to look like those of a pugilist." [2]

In one sense Crane's addiction to alcohol and to other dissipations was not unlike an addiction to narcotics. Behind each recurrence lurked some twisted promise of euphoria. But the promise was illusory, and the peace Crane sought always eluded him. It is one of the ironies of the man that the name he chose to use as a writer—Hart Crane—tended to call always to mind the two forces that may have contributed most to his condition. By choosing the surnames of his parents, he was also dramatizing in the focus of his own person the conflicting desires of which he was the single progeny.

Crane's problem of discovering a place for himself in his time only tended to complicate his personal ordeals as a poet. When he came to Cleveland after his experiences in Akron and Washington, he was attempting to resolve his personal problems for the first time on his own. Although the final result was not completely satisfactory, the Cleveland period was not without some value. Between April of 1922 and February of 1923, Crane composed all three parts of "For the Marriage of Faustus and Helen." His work on this poem helped him to integrate his own poetic talents as well as those influences which he derived from his study of the Elizabethans, the French Symbolist poets, Yeats, and Pound. In November of 1922, he was able to read Eliot's *The Wasteland* in *The Dial,* and Eliot's pessimistic indictment of the world of the twenties was to spur Crane's poetic ambitions more than any other poem which he read during that period. It is true that

[2] *On Modern Poets* (New York: Meridian, 1959).

8

he wrote to Munson to say he was "disappointed" in *The Wasteland,* adding that it was "good, of course, but so damned dead";
but he resolved to refute the *Weltschmerz* of Eliot's poem with
what he initially envisioned as a more optimistic poem about
America. In time this ambition, with certain modifications, was
to fructify in *The Bridge,* Crane's *magnum opus.*

❦

Crane was almost penurious when he quit his advertising job in
February, 1923. Despite a brief but heartening visit by Gorham
Munson, Crane continued to feel that he could perfect his talents
only in New York. When Munson and his wife subsequently
invited him to be their guest in their Greenwich Village apartment,
Crane eagerly accepted and moved back to New York.

Thriving on friendships new and renewed (with Matthew Jo-
sephson, then editor of the *Broom,* Padraic Colum, Waldo Frank,
Malcolm Cowley, Kenneth Burke, William Slater Brown, E. E.
Cummings, Eugene O'Neill, and others), Crane began to outline
and compose *The Bridge.* He originally envisioned it as a poem
that would not be more than twice the length of "For the Marriage
of Faustus and Helen." But his concept began to grow until it
far exceeded his first expectations. Soon his ambitions for *The
Bridge* became obsessions. All else became of subordinate interest
to him, and this had a negative effect upon several of his friends
and also upon his own efforts to support himself.

In finding a remunerative and compatible form of employment,
however, Crane was no more successful in New York than he had
been in Cleveland. Although he did find an advertising job with
Waldo Frank's assistance, it was not long before he felt that his
art was being compromised, and he resigned. The only difference,
perhaps, between this and earlier resignations from the many jobs
he had had, was his ability to be more philosophical about it. He
began to look with more perspicacity and not a little bitterness at
the dilemma in which he and some of his fellow artists seemed to
find themselves. In a letter to Charlotte Rychtarik in September,
he wrote:

> The situation for the artist in America seems to me to be getting
> harder and harder all the time. Most of my friends are worn out
> with the struggle here in New York. If you make enough to live
> decently on, you have no time left for your real work,—and other-
> wise you are constantly likely to starve.

9

After spending two months at Slater Brown's place in Woodstock, New York, Crane returned to the city in January, 1924. He received an unexpected check from his father and found brief advertising employ. Glorying in his new solvency, he moved into a room overlooking Brooklyn Bridge at 110 Columbia Heights, unaware that he was occupying the same room that Roebling, the bridge's designer, had lived in years before when his crippled state prevented him from working on the bridge any longer. Here for a while Crane found peace. At the same time his homosexuality asserted itself, and he invited a sailor to share the apartment— a relationship soon known to many. But his work on *The Bridge* progressed, and he was motivated to write the beautiful and moving "Voyages."

With critics like Allen Tate celebrating the achievement of "Voyages" and "For the Marriage of Faustus and Helen," Crane found a brief respite from desperation. But, when unemployment forced him to surrender his room, Slater Brown again offered him refuge, this time in the Berkshires in Patterson, New York. At the same time, Eugene O'Neill and Waldo Frank were trying to interest Horace Liveright in publishing a book of Crane's poems.

When the Liveright project failed and when his self-respect restrained him from leaning further on his friends, Crane returned to his former derelictions. For a time it seemed that his life had come to a complete halt. Then, in December, 1925, more out of chance than calculation, Crane wrote a letter to Otto Kahn, a New York banker and generous patron of needy artists, asking for a loan of one thousand dollars to continue his work on *The Bridge*. To Crane's surprise, Kahn responded with the amount asked for and a promise of another thousand in five-hundred dollar amounts.

Kahn's fortuitous advance enabled Crane to share the rental of a farmhouse (not far from the residence of Slater Brown) with Allen Tate and his wife, Caroline Gordon, in Patterson, New York, and despite occasional personality conflicts, Crane forged ahead on *The Bridge*. To strangers his methods of composition must have appeared unique. He had long since cultivated a Poe-like fondness for the muse of good whisky, but he now supplemented this with other idiosyncrasies. Malcolm Cowley has given a vivid description of these creative vagaries in his account of Crane during this period of his life:

> There would be a Sunday afternoon party on Tory Hill, near Patterson, New York, in Slater Brown's unpainted and unremodeled farmhouse. I can't remember any of the jokes that were made, or

why we laughed at them so hard; I can remember only the general atmosphere of youth and poverty and high spirits. Hart would be laughing twice as hard as the rest of us in the big, low-ceilinged kitchen; he would be drinking twice as much hard cider and contributing more than his share of the crazy metaphors and overblown epithets. Gradually he would fall silent and a little later we would find that he had disappeared. In lulls that began to interrupt the laughter, now Hart was gone, we would hear a new hubbub through the walls of the next room—the phonograph playing a Cuban rumba, the typewriter clacking simultaneously; then the phonograph would run down and the typewriter stop while Hart changed the record, perhaps to a torch song, perhaps to Ravel's "Bolero." Sometimes he stamped across the room, declaiming to the four walls and the slow spring rain. An hour later, after the rain had stopped, he would appear in the kitchen or on the croquet court, his face brick-red, his eyes burning, his already iron-gray hair bristling straight up from his skull. He would be chewing a five-cent cigar which he had forgotten to light. In his hands would be two or three sheets of typewritten manuscript, with words crossed out and new lines scrawled in. "Read that," he would say. "Isn't that the *grrrea*test poem ever written!" [3]

From the beginning the Patterson venture had none of the qualities of permanence. Shared chores were often allowed to slide, and the entire arrangement soon degenerated into acrimony. Crane suddenly remembered the vacation he had taken in 1915 to the Isle of Pines. It seemed the logical place to find the peace that had not been forthcoming in Patterson. Thus, in May, 1926, in company with Waldo Frank, Crane sailed for this island retreat on the S. S. "Orizaba," a ship that was destined to play a different role in his life a few years later.

Crane's stay on the Isle of Pines was both healthful and rewarding. While there, he learned that Horace Liveright had reconsidered his manuscript and finally decided to publish it under the title of *White Buildings*. This news spurred Crane's more extensive readings in the works of Herman Melville and Oswald Spengler. He resumed work on *The Bridge* with greater gusto and deepened his store of tropical imagery that would be woven into new lyrics. One critic, Louise Bogan, considers these short poems dealing with primitive tropical surroundings to be among his best. "The poems," she writes, "based on his experience of Caribbean islands, which display a wealth of natural detail against the ever-present background of a tragically realized tropic sea, show how

[3] *Exile's Return: A Literary Odyssey of the 1920's* (New York: Viking, 1951).

exquisitely the ardor of Crane's temperament could express itself when provided with sympathetic materials." [4]

Crane returned to New York in the fall, after the plantation was destroyed in a hurricane. The two-year period that followed was one of familiar patterns. Kahn's advance was gone, and only a new allotment of fifty dollars a month from his father sustained his poetic efforts, now reduced to the revision of some short poems written on the Isle of Pines. In May, 1927, he moved to Patterson and began "The River." In November he took a job as secretary to a stockbroker who was traveling to California, and it was there that he confessed to his mother, who was residing temporarily in Altemeda, his homosexual tendencies. Whether or not her reaction to this precipitated their increasing misunderstanding, Crane, in any case, resigned his position with the stockbroker and fled back to New York.

In New York Crane was successful in paying his debts only with his father's help, and his attempts to find steady work were in vain. His propensity for liquor continued, and the debauchery and disorder of his life grew. By this time the break with his mother was nearly final (worsened probably by his attempt to get five hundred dollars inheritance from the estate of his grandmother who died in September), and it was made permanent by his plans to leave for Europe.

The divided reaction of critics to his newly published *White Buildings* did little, meanwhile, to extricate him from his doldrums. Those who did not like the book belabored its ambiguity and condemned it on those grounds. Those who did praise it—Waldo Frank in *The New Republic,* Yvor Winters in *Poetry,* Allen Tate in his introductory essay to the book itself, and Mark Van Doren in *The Nation*—still felt a responsibility to defend what they considered to be the book's difficulties. Where Crane had expected accolades, he received either dismissal or guarded tribute; the result in either case was further disappointment. Even his subsequent successes in having poems published in *The Dial, Poetry, The Calendar, Transition, American Caravan,* and T. S. Eliot's *Criterion* were not enough to ameliorate his sense of artistic frustration. Work on *The Bridge* slackened and died except for the unexpected burst of energy that resulted in "The River."

In December, 1928, Crane sailed for Europe. His original intention was to settle on Majorca off the coast of Spain and finish

[4] *Achievement in American Poetry: 1900–1950* (Chicago: Henry Regnery, 1951).

work on *The Bridge*. But there was the lure of the Continent to reckon with. He stayed in London briefly and then went to France, where, except for a short trip to the south, he bogged down in the attractions of Paris and in the familiar cycle of drinking, arguing, and dissipating. A riot over his inability to pay a bill precipitated his return in July to the United States, where he lived for a time alternately between Patterson and Columbia Heights.

Somehow, he managed to complete three more sections of *The Bridge*—"Cape Hatteras," "Quaker Hill," and "Indiana"—and in October he sent these poems on to his friend, Harry Crosby, who intended to publish the work in its entirety at the Black Sun Press in Paris. Crosby's suicide delayed publication of the Black Sun edition, but the work was courageously brought to completion by Crosby's wife, Caresse. Crane was still unemployed when, finally in April, 1930, *The Bridge* appeared in the United States in the Liveright edition. The critical response of some critics was harsh (such as William Rose Benét's open ridicule in *The Saturday Review of Literature*), while the response of others was favorable (such as Granville Hick's review in *The Nation* and Vincent McHugh's in the *New York Evening Post*). But the more significant of the book's critics reflected the view of Allen Tate, Malcolm Cowley, and Yvor Winters that *The Bridge* represented an overextension of Crane's talents.

Crane's reaction to the antipathetic criticism of those men whose critical taste he valued was to defend *The Bridge* where he thought defense necessary, admit weakness where he thought it truly existed, and pledge himself to return to the more personal lyrics of *White Buildings*. The criticism of Benét he simply ignored.

In August, 1930, he applied to the Guggenheim Foundation for a fellowship to study in France. While awaiting response to this application, he found, with the help of Archibald MacLeish, interim employment as a feature writer for *Fortune* magazine. There, as in all his previous involvements with the world of business, he was repeatedly unsuccessful in completing the few writing assignments he was given. His homosexuality grew intense and his bouts of drunkenness multiplied. Often he was drunk for days.

In the spring of 1931, Crane received word that he had won the Guggenheim Fellowship, and he decided, for lack of a theme and upon the advice of friends, to study in Mexico, there to write an epic poem on the conquest of Mexico. Still, the news of the fellowship did not diminish his vices; it is also conceivable that the award may have had a completely negative effect on him, convincing him that only through patronage could he be rescued from poverty. In any case, he was completely intoxicated when he boarded ship and remained so until he reached Mexico City.

Mexico was to be the scene of his final undoing much as Paris in 1929 had been a preview of it. He stayed for awhile at the home of Katherine Anne Porter in Mixcoac, a suburb of Mexico City, then moved to the house next door, taking excursions once in a while to Taxco, an artists' colony, where much of the work on "The Broken Tower" was done. His Bohemianism not only alienated many of the Taxco townspeople but led some of Crane's friends to think he was verging on madness. From orgy to outburst to stupor Crane ventured along the path of self-destruction that was to culminate in his suicide less than a year later. Even the restraining influence of Katherine Anne Porter, who had also come to Mexico on a grant from the Guggenheim Foundation, did little to stabilize him. Crane's subsequent trip to the United States on the occasion of his father's death only served to delay what was to come. When Crane returned to Mexico, the pattern of his life in Mixcoac resumed.

Crane was never to finish the Mexican epic he had envisioned. Indeed, there is little evidence to suggest that he ever started it. He wrote a number of shorter poems, and there was a flash of his former power when he completed "The Broken Tower." But his output was uneven, and the Mexican poems, with only a few exceptions, are not among his best.

One of the final ironies of Crane's life was his eleventh hour attempt at romance. Shortly before his final departure from Mexico, Crane began to live with Peggy Baird, who was once the wife of Malcolm Cowley. Perhaps this was only a different aspect of Crane's twisted sexual perspective or perhaps he was making one last attempt to salvage some semblance of domestic peace from a life which had been denied the happiness of the usual familial relationships. However, Crane's relations with Peggy Baird were short-lived. After a brief interlude of comparative stability, he returned to his former habits. He frequently threatened to commit suicide, and on one occasion he slashed a portrait made of him by the Mexican artist David Siqueiros, after which he made an unsuccessful attempt to end his life by swallowing iodine. He became involved in recurrent saloon brawls, and there were times when his moments of violence approached insanity. Sometimes Crane would actually proclaim that he was Christ.

In this precarious state Crane advanced toward an almost predictable doom. Finally, following an urgent appeal from his stepmother to return to the United States to help her settle the litigation involved in his father's estate, Crane departed with Peggy Baird from Vera Cruz on April 24, 1932. The ship was the S. S. "Orizaba"—the same ship that had brought him to Mexico and, a few years before, had brought him to the idyllic peace of the Isle of Pines.

The few days Crane spent on board were to be as violent as the periodic eruptions of the volcano whose name the ship bore. Crane resumed his excessive drinking and there is one report that he was severely beaten after soliciting some members of the crew. His suicidal impulses became more and more apparent. On the second night out the night watch forcibly restrained Crane just as he was about to leap into the gulf. But what seemed to be a rescue was only a brief reprieve. On the morning of April 26, 1932, after a brief visit with Peggy Baird, Crane sauntered to the stern of the "Orizaba" and, in the sight of several passengers, climbed over the railing and leaped into the sea before anyone could stop him. After a futile search that lasted slightly more than one hour, the "Orizaba" resumed its journey to New York.

❧ ❧

It could be argued that Crane's suicide was a vindication of his own belief in suicide as a form of personal fulfillment. We know from an essay by Yvor Winters that Crane tended to regard suicide as "a great adventure." But the disintegration of Crane's personality was too long in the making to be redeemed by any final act of apparent heroism. Moreover, it is apparent to anyone conversant with the lifelong patterns of Crane's behavior that most of his vices were essentially self-destructive. His final leap from the "Orizaba" exceeded his homosexuality and his alcoholism not so much in intent as in degree. The end of each was self-destruction. Philip Horton, in his excellent biography of Crane, has come to a similar conclusion:

After tracing the course of his life and particularly the swift decline of the last years, beginning with the fall of 1927, there should be little need to insist upon the complex and organic character of his suicide. One may see it as an escape either from a society in which he had no function or from a psychic impasse which had no solution; one may see it morally as the violent issue of debauchery or, mystically, as the last desperate effort to achieve a transcendent unity through his favorite symbol, the sea; or finally, one may take a more general and inclusive view of it, such as the one so constantly stressed in these pages—namely, the lack of security, both spiritual and worldly, which, like an interior cavity hollowed by fear, distorted the surfaces and substrata of his life with fatal displacements.[5]

The end of Hart Crane's life bore out the pattern of his existence. Emotional instability, dissipation, and eventual abandonment of hope for his art seemed to precede this end. Biographical critics may discuss the relationship of his life to his work, and other critics may dispute it. There are few writers in American letters, nevertheless, whose lives can so impress their students with a sense of disappointment and tragedy.

[5] *Hart Crane: The Life of an American Poet* (New York: W. W. Norton, 1937).

◆§ NEW PURITIES

M OST of the critics who admire Crane's poetry are unanimously
high in their praise of his lyrical talent. And even those critics who have reservations about Crane's achievement as an American poet are usually willing to concede that he has written a dura-
ble number of short poems or that certain parts and lines of *The
Bridge* are notable lyrical moments.

Crane's versatility as a lyric poet in his first published book,
White Buildings, is best examined and most readily seen in stages.
The first stage would include those relatively simple poems which
reveal a strong influence of the Imagists. Crane's purpose in
these poems is the evocation of a single, dominant mood through
the use of sensation-creating tropes, as in "Legend," "My Grandmother's Love Letters," "Garden Abstract," "In Shadow," "The
Fernery," "North Labrador," "Pastorale," and "Sunday Morning
Apples." Included in the second stage are those poems in which
Crane is indebted to the Elizabethans and the French Symbolists,
as well as the Imagists. These are poems like "Black Tambourine" and "Stark Major" where Crane's imagistic ability fuses with
the careful conceits of the Elizabethans and the rapid, symbolic
transitions characteristic of Laforgue, Mallarmé and Rimbaud.
The third stage represents the fullest realization of Crane's lyrical
talent. The influences of the Imagists, the Elizabethans and the
French Symbolists are still apparent, but they are integrated into
and transcended by an idiom that is unmistakably Crane's own.

It is this aspect of Crane's talent that has led R. P. Blackmur to say that

> Crane habitually re-created his words from within, developing meaning to the point of idiom; and that habit is the constant and indubitable sign of talent. The meanings themselves are the idioms and have a twist and life of their own. It is only by ourselves meditating on and *using* these idioms—it is only by emulation—that we can master them and accede to their life.[1]

One finds this idiom in poems like "Praise for an Urn," "At Melville's Tomb," "Chaplinesque," "Lachrymae Christi," "Repose of Rivers," "Passage," "Paraphrase," "Possessions," "Recitative," "The Wine Menagerie," "For the Marriage of Faustus and Helen," and "Voyages."

Among the poems related to the imagistic stage of Crane's lyrical development is the first poem in *White Buildings*. "Legend" is not only a poem of affirmation but a synthesis of some of Crane's Platonic beliefs and poetic imperatives. Its theme evolves from the tension between death and renewal, giving and receiving, immolation and transfiguration.

In the opening lines of "Legend," Crane's vision of reality approximates the shadowed world of Plato's cave:

> As silent as a mirror is believed
> Realities plunge in silence by . . .

The world of reality is seen here as a reality of reflections, and it is believed and accepted just as mirrored images are accepted. But living in a reality of shadows does not engender despair in the poet. He does not renounce the world ("I am not ready for repentance"). On the contrary, he resolves to approach reality as closely as the "imploring flame" of life will permit. Moreover, it will be an approach suffused with love and a desire for renewal.

> And tremorous
> In the white falling flakes
> Kisses are,—
> The only worth all granting.

The section that follows this passage is the fulcrum of the poem:

> It is to be learned—
> This cleaving and this burning,
> But only by the one who
> Spends out himself again.

[1] *Language as Gesture* (New York: Harcourt, Brace, 1952).

The implication of this section, which capsulizes the theme of the poem, is that only the lover or giver is able to know the realities that "plunge in silence by." But the lover or giver is actually the poet who spends himself in and through his talent. The "cleaving" and "burning" are both images of desire and communion, which are related to the "moth" and "flame" images used in an earlier passage in the poem. By this linking of images the connection of poet and lover is given a symbolic unity.

Subsequent lines fulfill the imperative of this credo of love and fructification. The moth-lover-poet progression becomes first a "smoking souvenir" and then a "bleeding eidolon." Both of these images are suggestive of sacrifice or immolation; there is a slight but nonetheless definite overtone of the mystery of the phoenix in "smoking souvenir" and a suggestion of the Christ in "bleeding eidolon." The import of the entire passage seems to be that only through immolation does the being sacrificed embrace the "bright logic" of the "mirror" of life.

The suffering and communion that are symbolized by the painful shedding of blood ("drop by caustic drop") are what release the poet's awareness of beauty. But this release is possible only for the one who moves with faith into "the noon" of life. The noon-sun image suggests on the one hand the source of light that could project reflections of reality on the wall of Plato's cave. On the other hand it relates to the numberless meanings that the sun came to have for Crane—truth, inspiration, life itself. In the last stanza of "Legend" Crane integrates the image of blood (with its sacrificial associations) and the image of the sun (with its suggestions of vitality) in order to focus on the poem's dominant theme of regeneration through sacrifice:

> Then, drop by caustic drop, a perfect cry
> Shall string some constant harmony,—
> Relentless caper for all those who step
> The legend of their youth into the noon.

The technique of "Legend" is predominantly impressionistic. Crane came to rely on this technique more and more in his later poems but with added dimensions. At first, however, he was content to let the impressionism of his work reveal itself through a blending of imagery. But even in a poem like "Legend" one is able to see that Crane is already at work developing the technique of relating multiple images in a thematic progression, as in the development of the image of the moth into that of the lover and, finally, the poet.

This impressionistic technique also appears in a poem called "My Grandmother's Love Letters." Disregarding the biographical significance of this poem and subordinating for the moment the influences of Charles Vildrac, William Vaughn Moody, Paul Verlaine, and John Gould Fletcher that critics have discerned in it, the technique of composition is not unlike that of "Legend," although "My Grandmother's Love Letters" is a much less difficult poem to understand than "Legend."

"My Grandmother's Love Letters," which appeared in *The Dial*, is not only a poem of nostalgia but one which confronts the impossibility of man's attempts to revoke the onrush of time. Against the background of rainfall on a roof—a mocking but also an assuaging sound—the poet remembers

> . . . the letters of my mother's mother,
> Elizabeth,
> That have been pressed so long
> Into a corner of the roof
> That they are brown and soft
> And liable to melt as snow.

But the very act of probing into the past, that is as perishable in remembrance as the decomposing letters themselves, requires as much reverence as it does delicacy. The problem for the rememberer is further complicated by the insistence of the past in intruding upon the present.

> Over the greatness of such space
> Steps must be gentle.
> It is all hung by an invisible white hair.
> It trembles as birch limbs webbing the air.

Subsequently, the poet remonstrates with himself over the vanity of attempting to repossess the past. He suddenly recognizes that there have been too many interventions that would make any such recovery impossible regardless of his desire to lead his grandmother toward him through the starless night of "memory."

> Yet I would lead my grandmother by the hand
> Through much of what she would not understand;
> And so I stumble. And the rain continues on the roof
> With such a sound of gently pitying laughter.

The world of time and space suggested by the ticktock of raindrops serves to frame the timeless, spaceless desire of the poet within the limits of the possible. The "gently pitying laughter" of the rain is the final contradiction of the poet's attempt to win back the dead even through the means of memory.

Stylistically, "My Grandmother's Love Letters," like "Legend," shows Crane at an early stage of his development. The reliance upon imagery tends to dominate all other aspects of his talent. There is not the incipient impressionism of his *juvenilia*, but there is impressionism nonetheless. Edwin Honig's charge that Crane's mature work "often suffers from over-compression . . . on the side of technical modernisms"[2] cannot be corroborated in these early poems. There is not yet that compression and ingenious manipulation of symbol and image to lure critics like Honig to lodge such criticisms.

A poem similar in tone to "My Grandmother's Love Letters" but more sensual in mood and regular in form is "Garden Abstract." The original version of this poem was in the first person and in free verse. Crane's revision of the poem into its final, more regular form was undoubtedly made because of his propensity for the regularly metered line as opposed to what Robert Frost has called the netless tennis court of free verse. But Brom Weber has noted that Crane changed the poem from the first person to the third, not for aesthetic reasons, but because the phallic and even the homosexual implications of the first person version were embarrassingly called to his attention.

The allusion to the "apple" in the first line of "Garden Abstract" summons visions of Eden and the forbidden fruit. The woman in the poem gradually becomes another Eve within this new garden, and the tree from which the apple is suspended is converted into a masculine symbol.

> The apple on its bough is her desire,—
> Shining suspension, mimic of the sun.
> The bough has caught her breath up, and her voice,
> Dumbly articulate in the slant and rise
> Of branch on branch above her, blurs her eyes.
> She is prisoner of the tree and its green fingers.

In the second stanza Crane creates an abstract or myth in which the woman actually seems to *become* the tree, which has already been identified as the object of "her desire." The woman in effect submerges her identity in the object of her desire until she has achieved a sense of unity possible only through love.

[2] "American Poetry and the Rationalist Critic," *Virginia Quarterly* (Summer, 1960).

> And so she comes to dream herself the tree,
> The wind possessing her, weaving her young veins,
> Holding her to the sky and its quick blue,
> Drowning the fever of her hands in sunlight.
> She has no memory, nor fear, nor hope
> Beyond the grass and shadows at her feet.

Although this poem is certainly not among Crane's best, it shows how he was beginning to move in the direction of mythmaking and how his imagery was starting to move beyond the limits of the simple impressionistic lyric. These same beginnings are apparent in the five remaining poems that constitute this first stage in Crane's growth as a lyric poet: "In Shadow," "The Fernery," "North Labrador," "Pastorale," and "Sunday Morning Apples."

"In Shadow" is basically a love poem. It does not lean upon the mythical as heavily as "Garden Abstract," but there is still a mythical inclination. Of minor interest, but nonetheless relevant, is Crane's experimentation with prosody. Unwilling to go all the way with many of the Imagists in their fondness for free verse, Crane is willing to work almost exclusively within the bounds of the regular verse patterns.

> Out in the late amber afternoon,
> Confused among the chrysanthemums,
> Her parasol, a pale balloon,
> Like a waiting moon, in shadow swims.

The end rhymes of lines one and three, along with the rhyming sound appearing in the middle of line four, exemplify this. The structural inversion used to achieve this is especially admirable. It decelerates the movement of the entire stanza. This deceleration together with Crane's use of the back-vowel sounds contribute to the languor of the mood.

The second and third stanzas continue the description of the woman as she moves out of sunlight and back into shadow until she hears the footfalls of her lover.

> Gently yet suddenly, the sheen
> Of stars inwraps her parasol.
> She hears my step behind the green
> Twilight, stiller than shadows, fall.

Perhaps Crane should have ended the poem here. It is certainly thematically complete at this point. The fourth stanza, which intrudes the words of the lover upon an already realized scene and mood, seems not only anticlimactic but superfluous.

"The Fernery" is an example of an imagistic poem used allegorically. The subject of the poem is a woman in concentration. The "spectacles" she wears are shields or mere light-reflectors. In this moment of introspection she is hardly aware of them as glasses at all. Only the pursed lips and the lines around her mouth reveal the intensity of her thinking.

> The lights that travel on her spectacles
> Seldom, now, meet a mirror in her eyes.
> But turning, as you may chance to lift a shade
> Beside her and her fernery, is to follow
> The zigzags fast around dry lips composed
> To darkness through a wreath of sudden pain.

"Darkness" and "fresh sunlight" are contrasted as the second stanza begins. This contrast sharpens the difference between the internal world of the perplexed woman and the tranquility of her surroundings. The very tidiness of her semblance contrasts pointedly with her self-preoccupation. Her inner confusion is made even more intense for the reader by her "merciless tidy hair." This carefully elaborated contrast is converted in the final lines of the poem into an allegory for the observing poet's similar state or mood. The poet knows the same discrepancy between his "confusions" and the apparent neatness of the world around him.

> —So, while fresh sunlight splinters humid green
> I have known myself a nephew to confusions
> That sometimes take up residence and reign
> In crowns less grey—O merciless tidy hair!

Crane again relies upon contrast to realize the mood of "North Labrador." He describes the dominant frigidity of the scene with images that are obviously erotic. The poem itself is self-explanatory, but what saves it from being a mere description of arctic wastes is the central stanza. Here Crane goes beyond mere contrast. In a protracted rhetorical question Crane confronts the land of Labrador as if he were addressing an isolated woman forever beyond desire or change. With the land of perpetual winter thus personified, the poem presents a dramatic contrast between desire and sterility.

> "Has no one come here to win you,
> Or left you with the faintest blush
> Upon your glittering breasts?
> Have you no memories, O Darkly Bright?"

In "Pastorale" and "Sunday Morning Apples" Crane shows inclinations to move from the imagistic to the symbolic. Both poems should be regarded as transitions between the first and second stages of Crane's lyrical development. "Pastorale" expresses the poet's regret over the inevitable passing of summer. But the death of summer receives no more grandiose particularization than the symbol of a withered bouquet of violets. The poem progresses to this last symbolic image with an abruptness appropriate to summer's sudden termination. The symbol is left isolated in a sharp fade-out of meter.

> "Fool—
> Have you remembered too long;
>
> Or was there too little said
> For ease or resolution—
> Summer scarcely begun
> And violets,
> A few picked, the rest dead?"

"Sunday Morning Apples," which is addressed and dedicated to an artist-lithographer whom Crane knew in Cleveland, is more than simply a tribute to the art of William Sommer. By considering the apples in Sommer's painting as symbols of art objects generally, it is possible to interpret the poem as a tribute to the transfigurative character of all art.

Crane begins the poem with a reference to the "rich and faithful strength of line" of Sommer's technique. After this brief exposition the poem builds to the climax of the final lines. Crane contemplates the apples in a still-life prop and wonders how they will reveal their "secrets" to the painter when he becomes engaged in capturing their beauty on canvas. Pursuing this thought, Crane concludes that the painter will paint apples more real than the apples in actual fact. He will select and transfigure until he seizes the inner reality of the apples. The abruptness of the final line of the poem directs our attention to this aesthetic fact.

> I have seen the apples there that toss you secrets,—
> Beloved apples of seasonable madness
> That feed your inquiries with aerial wine.
> Put them again beside a pitcher with a knife,
> And poise them full and ready for explosion—
> The apples, Bill, the apples!

The two most representative poems of Crane's second lyrical stage are "Black Tambourine" and "Stark Major." The Imagist

24

influences are supplemented in both poems by techniques which Crane gleaned from his study of Marlowe, Jonson, Drayton, Mallarmé, Laforgue, and Huysmans. In "Black Tambourine," for example, Crane is not averse to adapting a semi-Marlovian rhetoric to his treatment of a subject drawn from modern times. Elsewhere he relies more and more upon the symbol and the symbolic metaphor. It is left to the imagination of the reader to supply the many transitions that Crane has deliberately omitted.

This is not to say that Crane was henceforth to be free of all literary influences but these or that he would from the early twenties onward succeed without interruption in adapting these influences and others to an idiom that was uniquely his. Even in the middle twenties Crane was to write a few poems that were to imitate to the point of mimicry the techniques of poets he admired. But these poems are really not in the line of his true development. A poem like "Emblems of Conduct," which Crane wrote after he had obtained possession of the manuscript of an obscure poet named Samuel Greenberg, is interesting primarily as a tangent. According to Weber, "Emblems of Conduct," which was written in 1924 when Crane was involved with such original creations as "Lachrymae Christi," "Recitative," and "Voyages," is practically "a complete transmutation of lines taken from several Greenberg poems." No such mimicry is apparent in either "Black Tambourine" or "Stark Major."

The status of the Negro in early twentieth-century America is the subject of "Black Tambourine." The dominant picture in the poem is the "mid-kingdom" that the Negro inhabits. If there is some sociological coloring in this phrase, it is there in a factual rather than in a political or propagandist sense. In a letter to Gorham Munson, Crane has said that "mid-kingdom" bears upon the "Negro's place somewhere between man and beast" not in an evolutionary but a sociological sense, and the poem reflects this interpretation.

The image that concretizes the "Negro's place" in the poem is that of the Negro in a cellar. The subterranean atmosphere serves to emphasize the limbo-like quality of his existence. But the true meaning of "mid-kingdom" emerges from Crane's contrast of the "black tambourine" of the present, which symbolizes the minstrel-like picture of the Negro in the public mind, with the primitive, original habitat suggested by the decaying "carcass" in Africa. The "tardy judgment" is essentially the comment that the existential "interests" of the Negro make upon the historical past of

25

his African origins as well as upon the prejudice ("the world's closed door") which confronts him in the present. The "closed door" of misrepresentation and nonacceptance thus keeps the Negro midway between the *then* of a human though primitive heritage and the *now* of a subhuman social status. Against this background the allusion to Aesop, who was himself a slave, becomes ironic. The grave of Aesop, which is a counterpart of the "closed door" of the black man's "mid-kingdom" existence, has been overlooked. It is hidden under "fox brush" and "sow ear." But the wisdom of Aesop has outlived such negligence. Like the "tortoise" in his own fable, Aesop has beaten the "hare" of time, and his name survives by persisting in the "mingling incantations on the air."

Clues of Crane's maturation as a lyric poet are evident in "Black Tambourine" in the flexibility of diction and image, the functional reversals and substitutions within the traditionally regular verses of the poem, and the abrupt shifts of focus from stanza to stanza without transitional aids. Crane is literally daring the imagination of the reader to make the transitions that he has not written into the poem in order to heighten the impact of each of the three stanzas as they are read.

The style of "Black Tambourine" suggests that Crane had reached a truce with impressionism when he wrote the poem. He was willing to use impressionistic devices but only within the bounds established by his own propensities for metrical regularity and for the riches of metaphors and symbols. "Black Tambourine" is a step beyond impressionism. It is Crane's commitment to avoid Dadaism, which he regarded as the "dying agonies" of the impressionistic movement. At this stage in his career Crane was not moving ahead by accident or luck. He knew exactly where he was going.

Of "Stark Major" Crane said in a letter to Munson, "I can't quite justify the title in words, but it came to me quite freely as the right thing." Just as Crane felt that the title for "Stark Major" was "the right thing," so did he trust that perceptive readers like Munson would "get it." This tends to validate an observation by Blackmur quoted earlier in this chapter. Blackmur noted that one sign of Crane's maturation was his propensity to re-create "his words from within" and that only our "meditating" on them can help us to "master them and accede to their life." Such meditation may or may not provide us with a helpful paraphrase or rationale. "Stark Major"—considered only as a title—does not lend itself to easy definition. It is as if Crane were reaching to strike an ultimate chord of life itself and that only the juxtaposition of these two words could capture it with a sense of finality.

Despite the tantalizing ambiguity of the title, the poem itself is relatively free of vexing obscurities. The poem's central situation is a moment of leave-taking. A lover is making his departure from a woman described in an unspecified but nonetheless unmistakable stage of pregnancy—"Her mound of undelivered life/Lies cool upon her—not yet pain." The "lifting spring" of approaching daylight prompts the departing lover to speculate upon the vivisecting torpor of the day ahead before his return in the evening when he and his beloved will again be united.

> Not yet is there that heat and sober
> Vivisection of more clamant air
> That hands joined in the dark will answer
> After the daily circuits of its glare.

The first line of the third stanza contains the phrase that is the crux of the poem's meaning—"the time of sundering." The immediate implication of the phrase is that the lover's farewell brings about a time of physical separation or "sundering" of lover and beloved. Their night of being together has come to an end. But the line is also prophetic of the separation that the imposing fact of childbirth will necessitate. The lovers may desire to be together, but the actual bearing of the child will of necessity be a private act from which the man will be excluded in more than a physical sense. Weber has suggested in his critique of the poem that this theme is enforced by the setting of the poem as well, noting that "the birth of a child (like the birth of day) inevitably separates the two lovers who have conceived it, and emphasizes the suffering of the lover who is thinking the thoughts that compose the poem."

The consequences of the separation of the two lovers unfold in the fourth and subsequent stanzas of the poem. The woman remains "beneath the green silk counterpane" and contemplates the impending drama of birth. The lover leaves to confront his death as a "lover." He will look at "doors and stone with broken eyes" because he has been in a sense left behind, while the woman has been precipitated toward experiences he "cannot ever reach to share." Her memories will be of things proper to any woman about to bring a human being into the world. This experience is granted to her by nature, but it is denied the lover. Ironically, her anticipation of new life is what creates the lover's ennui and marks the beginning of his death as a lover.

A. Alvarez has given a different interpretation of "Stark Major." Alvarez contends that the poem "explores the situation—the girl dead, the lover departing." [3] If Alvarez is insisting that the girl is dead, it is difficult to find evidence for the death of the girl in the poem. Moreover, it is even more difficult to interpret the meaning of death in anything but a symbolic manner. Neither the girl nor the lover actually *dies* in the poem. What dies is a former way of life for both people, nothing more.

The poems in the third stage of Crane's lyrical development reveal the true Hart Crane. In these poems he has integrated his talents and influences so that the voice we hear is definitely his own. The rhetoric is there, but it is no longer Marlovian; it is Crane's. The symbolic metaphors are there, but they are no longer the metaphors of Verlaine or Laforgue; they are Crane's. The blank verse is no longer a mimicry of the blank verse of the great Elizabethans; it is Crane's.

In poems like "Praise for an Urn" and "At Melville's Tomb" Crane is a poet in complete possession of his powers. It is not surprising, therefore, that these two poems, which are the only two elegies in *White Buildings,* have received the approval of Crane's critics as among the best poems that he ever wrote.

"Praise for an Urn" is dedicated to a Norwegian lithographer named Ernest Nelson, whom Crane met through William Sommer during his stay in Cleveland in the early twenties and who died and was cremated in 1922. Crane saw in Nelson a symbol of his own condition as an artist. Crane's proclivity for seeing his problems prefigured in others was not uncommon; his love for the art of Charlie Chaplin, for example, was due in great part to the fact that Chaplin's clown personified much of the pathos of the eternally misunderstood and victimized man. At any rate, Crane perceived in Nelson a counterpart of his own suffering as an American artist. Nelson's interests in painting and poetry had gradually been subordinated to the hard and more pressing facts of earning his living, which compelled him to devote all his time to lithography. Crane was undergoing a similar crisis during his stay in Cleveland, and he could appreciate Nelson's dilemma as his own.

Prompted not only by his real friendship for Nelson but also by his sympathy for his brother-artist's plight, Crane wrote "Praise for an Urn" as Nelson's poetic epitaph, grafting into the poem, as

[3] *Stewards of Excellence* (New York: Scribner's, 1958).

was his lifelong poetic practice, lines that he wrenched from an early and much less successful poem called "The Bridge of Estador."

The first stanza of "Praise for an Urn" emphasizes not only Nelson's Scandinavian ancestry ("kind and northern face") but also suggests something of his temperament in a symbolic, fecund reference to Pierrot, the classical harlequin with the "everlasting" merry-and-sad eyes, and Gargantua, the Rabelaisian giant of *La Vie Très Horrifique du Grand Gargantua*. The timeless "eyes of Pierrot" and the "laughter" of Gargantua are "mingled" in the "exile guise" of Nelson. The adjective "exile" tends to universalize Nelson as the pilgrim-artist, the eternal seeker, the wanderer or, in a larger sense, as man himself.

> His thoughts, delivered to me
> From the white coverlet and pillow,
> I see now, were inheritances—
> Delicate riders of the storm.

Nelson's last words—"delivered" from the deathbed of "white coverlet and pillow"—are regarded in retrospect ("I see now") as the dying man's spiritual legacies to his friend. The poet-friend now sees these legacies ("thoughts") as destined to outlast the "storm" of time and suffering and possibly life itself.

The allusion to the "slant moon on the slanting hill" is more than an image of place. On one level, of course, it can be accepted as a description of a scene once contemplated by Nelson and Crane. But the image suggests declivity and can thus be easily related to archetypal images suggestive of the passage of time. It is also possible that the moon could be a symbol of death or some other macabre omen to contrast with the life-symbol of the sun in the very last line of the poem. If so, the image of the moon serves a dual purpose. First, it suggests place; second, it creates the atmosphere of impending death. It is probable that this mood of impending death brought home to both men certain "presentiments" or premonitions of immortality—"what the dead keep, living still." It is also probable that this mood gave them a truer perspective of the world of fact, helping them to realize how few are the "glories" capable of being achieved in time.

In stanza four the clock in the "crematory lobby," by recording the passing of the temporal moment, comments derisively upon these meditations having to do with life and afterlife. The clock is time militating against the desires of two men to transcend it.

It intrudes to mock their ambitions. After we finish the fourth stanza, we are aware of little beyond the sound of the clock in the crematory. We are brought face to face with the clock so abruptly in a scenic contrast from the "slanting hill" to the "lobby" of the crematory that we feel ourselves conceding that time is possibly the only victor after all. As victor, it comments upon the defeat of even the noblest human ambitions just as the moon on the "slanting hill" presaged the limitations and the decline of human "glories."

> Still, having in mind gold hair,
> I cannot see that broken brow
> And miss the dry sound of bees
> Stretching across a lucid space.

In this stanza Crane remembers the man as he was prior to death. The allusion to "gold hair" can be interpreted at one level as a literal description of the color of Nelson's hair. But "gold hair" is one of Crane's favorite symbols for love or friendship. It appears, for example, with the same connotation in the final line of the penultimate stanza of "For the Marriage of Faustus and Helen" and in at least three other poems. Weber has suggested that Crane's choice of "gold hair" as a symbol of love may have stemmed from the fact that "many of the people whom Crane loved, including his mother, had gold hair." This may or may not be true, but, whenever the image of "gold hair" appears in one of Crane's poems, the symbolic linking of love and "gold hair" is strongly implied. The "broken brow" could possibly be an allusion to the sense of defeat which Nelson knew as an artist. This simple image could easily be Crane's poetic counterpart of a passage from a letter which he wrote shortly after Nelson's death:

> Nelson was a Norwegian who rebelled against the religious restrictions of home and came to America when a mere kid. As soon as he was through school, an aunt of his in America . . . forced him into the prostitution of all his ideals and a cheap lithographic work that he was never able to pull out of afterward. He wrote several good poems published in *Scribner's* & *Century* a long time ago, got married, and I finally met him here in Cleveland where he had been living in seclusion for a number of years. One of the best-read people I ever met, wonderful kindliness and tolerance and a true Nietzschean. He was one of many broken against the stupidity of American life in such places as here

The image of "the dry sound of bees/Stretching across a lucid space" is indeed obscure. Like many of Crane's images, this image is one of suggestion and is best understood by explaining what it suggests in the context of the poem. However, the image can be regarded as an attempt by Crane to suggest an intellectual frontier buzzing with thought. It could also be a symbol of Nelson's busy life as a lithographer in contrast with the lucidity of his unrealized artistic ideals. Both of these interpretations are, of course, highly subjective, but neither is inconsistent with the development of the poem's theme nor with the limits established by the words themselves.

The final stanza is almost an epitaph in itself:

> Scatter these well-meant idioms
> Into the smoky spring that fills
> The suburbs, where they will be lost.
> They are no trophies of the sun.

Crane here wishes the "well-meant idioms" of the poem he has written scattered (perhaps like the cremated man's ashes) into the "smoky spring" of the "suburbs." A shabby renascence is suggested by "smoky spring," which could also be symbolic of the befuddlement and opaque character of certain aspects of city life where poetic requiems for unknown artists like Nelson "will be lost." Is Crane saying that words themselves, however "well-meant" they may be, can never really be an adequate souvenir of life? Is the last stanza something of an anticlimax? Is there a note of futility about it, of abandonment, of capitulation to the victorious and unhaltable clock?

From a technical point of view "Praise for an Urn" is enriched by a number of significant contrasts. First, there is the contrast of the bittersweet and Pagliacci-like humanity of Pierrot with the raucous laughter of Gargantua. This is followed by the image of the final "thoughts" of a dying man which are capable of becoming "riders of the storm." There is the implied but omnipresent urn of human ashes contrasted with the remembered "gold" of Nelson's hair. Finally, there is the central paradox of the poem itself as an attempt to remember a dead man "living still" against the implied futility of the poet's trying to commemorate anything at all. This paradox is developed further in the image of futile sunlight in a "smoky spring," which links with the smoke from incineration and cremation and thereby relates to the scattering of the poet's "well-meant idioms" like so much ashes from the dying fire of the poem-memoir. These involved contrasts are not unique to "Praise for an Urn." They are more or less typical of all of the poems in this third stage of Crane's lyricism.

One of the best defenses of the techniques used in the second elegy, "At Melville's Tomb," is contained in a letter written by Crane to Harriet Monroe, who, in her capacity as editor of *Poetry* magazine, was considering the poem for publication pending Crane's answers to certain questions she had made about it. Crane's answer might be regarded by some as an apology for the poem in the intentionalist sense. But he is really not concerned with the relationship between intention and fact. The focus is truly critical. He does not attempt an explanation of what he was striving to do but concentrates on the metaphorical principles that prompted what he actually did:

> My poem may well be elliptical and actually obscure in the order-ing of its content, but in your criticism of this very possible de-ficiency you have stated your objections in terms that allow me, at least for the moment, the privilege of claiming your ideas and ideals as theoretically, at least, quite outside the issues of my own aspirations. To put it more plainly, as a poet I may very pos-sibly be more interested in the so-called illogical impingements of the connotation of words on the consciousness (and their combina-tions and interplay in metaphor on this basis) than I am interested in the preservation of their logically rigid significations at the cost of limiting my subject matter and perceptions involved in the poem. . . . It all comes to the recognition that emotional dy-namics are not to be confused with any absolute order of rational-ized definitions; ergo, in poetry the *rationale* of metaphor belongs to another order of experience than science, and is not to be limited by a scientific and arbitrary code of relationships either in verbal inflections or concepts.

The fact that Crane felt obligated to explain the *"rationale"* or "logic" of metaphor may seem a superfluous or merely academic matter to many. But poetic defenses are almost as old as poetry itself, and, when regarded as ancillary to the poems themselves, they can help us understand the poet's method and idiom. This is especially true of "At Melville's Tomb," which relies strongly on "illogical impingements of the connotations of words" to com-municate its meaning.

> Often beneath the wave, wide from this ledge
> The dice of drowned men's bones he saw bequeath
> An embassy. Their numbers as he watched
> Beat on the dusty shore and were obscured.
>
> And wrecks passed without sound of bells,
> The calyx of death's bounty giving back

A scattered chapter, livid hieroglyph,
The portent wound in corridors of shells.

Then in the circuit calm of one vast coil,
Its lashings charmed and malice reconciled,
Frosted eyes there were that lifted altars;
And silent answers crept across the stars.

Compass, quadrant and sextant contrive
No farther tides . . . High in the azure steeps
Monody shall not wake the mariner.
This fabulous shadow only the sea keeps.

The interpretation given the basic theme of this poem by
Cleanth Brooks and Robert Penn Warren is, though brief, an adequate and representative one. "The poet says," they conclude,
"that the spirit of the writer whose imagination was so vividly
engaged by the sea, and who saw such grandeur in man's struggle
with it, though his body might be buried on land, would find its
real abiding place in the sea." [4] By integrating the Brooks and
Warren interpretation of the sea as Melville's "tomb" with Crane's
explanation of the poem's "logic of metaphor" it is possible to
analyze the poem so that it readily yields its meaning.

In the first stanza the poet pictures Melville as the latter stands
on a "ledge" and watches the bones of drowned crews of nameless
ships cast up like "dice" on an underwater reef. These random,
anonymous bones bear a message ("embassy") to the observer.
This message may be the testament of man's eternal struggle with
the sea. It may be a revelation of his need to challenge the oceans
with ships even though he knows that he may never return and
that only his skeletal remnants, washed upon a "dusty shore,"
may be the final evidence of his quest.

As the poem proceeds, the observer (Melville) seems to hear the
ghosts of the wrecked ships passing "without sound of bells." The
subsiding "calyx" or whirlpool which has cast up the flotsam and
jetsam of these derelicts (reminiscent perhaps of the doomed
Pequod of Melville's *Moby Dick*) then yields its message to both
the eye and ear. Visually, we are confronted with the "scattered
chapter, livid hieroglyph" of bobbing driftwood that gives a floating picture-story of the ill-starred journeys. Then Crane trans-
forms the metaphor until we are aware of the "calyx" as a huge
conch which yields its "portent" to the hearer. The "corridors"

[4] *Understanding Poetry* (New York: Holt, 1960).

can easily be synonymous with the echoing convolutions of a sea shell held next to the ear.

The third stanza is stylistically related to some of Crane's more ambitious sea imagery in such longer poems as "Voyages" and "Ave Maria." With "lashings charmed and malice reconciled," the "calm" and "coil" of the sea becomes a transparent cover over the uplifted eyes of drowned seamen. We receive an overtone of a Shakespearian "sea-change" in Crane's allusion to "frosted eyes." Pictured as if in prayer, the drowned men look up eternally as if in expectation of some cosmic answer from the "stars."

In the final stanza the dirge reaches its climax. The poet claims that in death the conventional instruments of navigation can "contrive/No farther tides." This metaphor has a dual meaning. The first and most apparent meaning is that all earthly boundaries are nullified by death; therefore, "compass, quadrant and sextant" are simply no longer useful. The second meaning is that such nautical instruments can chart no tides "farther" than those of eternity itself. From the eternity of the "azure steeps" no poem of mourning can call the dead back to life ("wake the mariner"). It may be worth noting that Melville's own poem, "Monody," may have had something to do with Crane's incorporation of that word into the penultimate line of the final stanza. The poet then concludes the elegy by locating the seafaring spirit of Melville within the sea itself—his most appropriate tomb.

Of equal critical interest to a total appreciation of the poem is Crane's prosody. The rhymes, though irregularly patterned in the three stanzas in which rhyme appears, still serve the integrative purpose for which rhyme itself exists. But the metrical variations and the skillful manipulation of tonal and alliterative effects contribute more functionally to the poem's meaning. The hovering accent in "wide from" in line one of the first stanza is perfectly suited to a sense of vastness, and the trochaic substitution in the first foot of the fourth line places the stress directly upon the important, onomatopoeic word "beat." There are also such effectively balanced lines as the second line in the third stanza which gives equal emphasis to "lashings" and "malice." Finally, the rapid diminuendo on the phrase "without sound of bells" is like a suddenly muted chord, and the spondaic character of "one vast coil" suggests the breadth of the sea itself.

Another elegy of sorts is Crane's "Chaplinesque." Elegiac in tone toward a human type or a human propensity rather than toward a particular person, Crane directs his poetic attention to

what was symbolized by Chaplin's famous clown. The choice of
Chaplin's clown was not a haphazard one. In Chaplin's clown he
saw not only a burlesque Pagliacci but also something of the poet.
Chaplin's antics personified the "buffooneries of the tragedian" to
Crane, and a struggling poet like Crane could all too readily iden-
tify himself with such "buffooneries."

The extent of Crane's admiration for Chaplin is brought out
in a letter which he wrote to Gorham Munson from Cleveland in
October, 1921:

> And I must tell you that my greatest dramatic treat since seeing
> Garden in *The Love of Three Kings* two winters ago, was recently
> enjoyed when Charlie Chaplin's *The Kid* was shown here. Comedy,
> I may say, has never reached a higher level in this country before.
> We have . . . in Chaplin a dramatic genius that truly approaches
> the fabulous sort. I could write pages on the overtones and bril-
> liant subtleties of this picture, for which nobody but Chaplin can
> be responsible, as he wrote it, directed it.—and I am quite sure had
> much to do with the settings which are unusually fine.

Crane's admiration for Chaplin was given a boost two years later
when poet and actor met in New York. This was, of course, long
after Crane completed "Chaplinesque" and has only a tangential
relationship to it.

> We make our meek adjustments,
> Contented with such random consolations
> As the wind deposits
> In slithered and too ample pockets.
>
> For we can still love the world, who find
> A famished kitten on the step, and know
> Recesses for it from the fury of the street,
> Or warm torn elbow coverts.
>
> We will sidestep, and to the final smirk
> Dally the doom of that inevitable thumb
> That slowly chafes its puckered index toward us,
> Facing the dull squint with what innocence
> And what surprise!
>
> And yet these fine collapses are not lies
> More than the pirouettes of any pliant cane;
> Our obsequies are, in a way, no enterprise.
> We can evade you, and all else but the heart:
> What blame to us if the heart live on.

> The game enforces smirks; but we have seen
> The moon in lonely alleys make
> A grail of laughter of an empty ash can,
> And through all sound of gaiety and quest
> Have heard a kitten in the wilderness.

It came as a mild shock to Crane that some of those to whom he showed "Chaplinesque" thought it obscure. Crane was not above admitting that he thought the poem difficult, but he balanced this by saying that "Chaplinesque" was a new letter in the developing alphabet of his art and that this alphabet was comprehensible to those who took the time to learn it. When told that the poem was "most difficult," Crane only felt a confirmation of the sense that "he was approaching the creation of a personal idiom which in its language and technique would be indubitably an expression of his own temperament." According to Horton, Crane replied to the more severe critics of the poem "by confessing that its technique was 'virtuosic' and open to misunderstanding and that it failed to express its meaning to any but a very few readers."

The "virtuosic" qualities of "Chaplinesque" derive principally from its abrupt transitions and from the symbolic overtones of the images of the kitten and the clown. These qualities are appropriate to the third stage of Crane's lyrical development. They make demands upon the reader to be sure, but they are legitimate demands. The serious reader must attune himself to them as he must attune himself to the very texture of Crane's developing poetic vocabulary, which is as much concerned with a word's pigment and sound as with its meaning. F. O. Matthiessen has written that Crane "followed the French Symbolists in regarding words plastically, in treating them as though they had shapes and colors which must make an 'impact on the imagination.' " [5] This describes the linguistic texture of "Chaplinesque" perfectly. But the impact Crane hoped for was lost on many who were used to poems that were more explicit in their statement. Yet, he did not allow himself to be deterred. His study of the Symbolists (he took great pride in his halting translations of several poems of Laforgue) only intensified his reliance upon the plasticity of language and encouraged him, in the words of Leonard Unger and William Van O'Connor, to go on

> finding unusual relationships between objects; making evocative statements as opposed to explicit statements; exploring the con-

[5] *Dictionary of American Biography* (New York: Scribner's, 1944).

notative meanings of words rather than relying on denotative meanings; exploring the range of associations both personal and general, implicit in a coherent body of imagery; depending upon synaesthesia, or the unifying and exchanging of sense impressions; and moving from meaning to meaning within the poem by relying on association rather than strict logic.[6]

In "Chaplinesque" Crane was daring the imaginations of his readers at these levels of expression.

Keeping in mind the dominant figure of Chaplin's clown and its symbolic significance as a prototype of man as poet, it is not far-fetched to say that Crane's use of the plural personal pronoun in the first line of the poem is not only a way of identifying himself with the clown but of indicating that he, as poet, is speaking for all mankind. It is man in the collective sense who makes his "meek adjustments" and who finds contentment in "random consolations" brought to him by the "winds" of chance and change. Similarly, it is man whose very humanity will not permit him to overlook the "famished kitten on the step." The kitten is an appropriate symbol of those things which beguile our affection and thus implicate us in their plight by an appeal to our sympathy and love. It stands for everything which forces us to be "human" whether we will it or not. The clown, whom Crane regarded as "the poet in U.S.A. today," is drawn to protect the "kitten" in the "torn elbow coverts" of his kindness. In a letter written to William Wright from Cleveland in 1921, Crane has given similar elaborations to these overtones in the poem:

> I am moved to put Chaplin with the poets (of today); hence the "we." In other words, he . . . made me feel myself, as a poet, as being "in the same boat" with him. Poetry, the human feelings, "the kitten," is so crowded out of the humdrum, rushing, mechanical scramble of today that the man who would preserve them must duck and camouflage for dear life to keep them or keep himself from annihilation.

Armed only with the "final smirk" of personal protest, the clown is able to confront the policeman, who is a symbol of fate as well as of man-created controls, with characteristic "innocence" and "surprise." He thus attempts continually to "sidestep" or squirm from beneath the accusation of the "thumb" of fate and to avoid the scorn of authority's "dull squint."

One of the most difficult words to explicate within the context

[6] *Poems for Study* (New York: Rinehart, 1953).

of the fourth stanza is "obsequies." An obsequy is literally a fu-
neral rite of some importance. Yet Crane states that the "obsequies" of clown· man-poet "are, in a way, no enterprise." Does
this mean that the death rites of human beings are actually of
trivial importance? If this is Crane's meaning, we easily are
drawn to the conclusion that one of the themes of the poem is that
death is as inescapable as the impulses of the heart. We cannot
blame the clown, therefore, for harboring the symbolic kitten any
more than we could blame him for dying. Sympathy and death,
according to this interpretation, are equally integral to the nature
and destiny of man. He can with some guile or luck evade cir-
cumstance (fate) or authority, but he cannot evade his own humanity. But Crane might have erred in his use of this word. We
know that he was at times guilty of lapses or distortions of usage
even in his best poems. Could he, therefore, have mistaken "obsequies" for the substantive form of "obsequious?" If "obsequies" is such a lapse or distortion, then the clown could easily
have been regarded as obsequious before the policeman. Chaplin
himself frequently acted in this way in similar cinematographic
situations. Such clownish apologies could easily have come to be
regarded by Crane as "no enterprise."

The concluding stanza fulfills what is suggested by "what blame
to us if the heart live on." Because of man's inability to betray
the imperatives of his own heart and because the imperatives of
the heart often force him into positions where he must make "meek
adjustments," he often lapses into "smirks." The "game" of life
is played for such stakes. Yet even in bitterness, there is left to
man some consciousness of beauty and joy ("grail of laughter")
and also of love ("kitten in the wilderness").

"Lachrymae Christi" typifies the extremes to which Crane could
go at this third stage of his development. The range of association is so daring here that it becomes at times simply puzzling.
The transitions are so abrupt that they tend to mystify.

One of the most revealing critiques of the poem has been written by Martin Staples Shockley.[7] Beginning with a discussion of
the contrast between pastoral and industrial imagery at the beginning of the poem, Shockley proceeds to relate "thorns" and "the
year's/First blood" and "flanks unfended" to the eloquent tears
of the sacrificed Christ. Like Dionysus, Christ is able to triumph
through sacrifice.

[7] "Hart Crane's 'Lachrymae Christi,' " *University of Kansas City Review*
(Autumn, 1949).

Names peeling from Thine eyes
And their undimming lattices of flame,
Spell out in palm and pain
Compulsions of the year, O Nazarene.

Lean long from sable, slender boughs,
Unstanched and luminous. And as the nights
Strike from Thee perfect spheres,
Lift up in lilac-emerald breath the grail
Of earth again—
                    Thy face
From charred and riven stakes, O
Dionysus, Thy
Unmangled target smile.

Whether or not Crane thought "Lachrymae Christi" a poem that could justifiably be called difficult is unknown. It is significant to note, however, that he never wrote another poem exactly like it. Perhaps he felt that he had taken too inordinate a gamble with the sensitivity and imagination of even his most sympathetic readers. The remaining poems in *White Buildings* that are at this third level of Crane's lyrical development—"Repose of Rivers," "Passage," "Paraphrase," "Possessions," "Recitative," "The Wine Menagerie," "For the Marriage of Faustus and Helen," and "Voyages"—are, though difficult, not quite as puzzling in their idiom or their development as "Lachrymae Christi."

"Repose of Rivers" derives its basic force from a combination of reminiscence and contrast. Almost Wordsworthian in its tranquility, the theme of the poem emerges from the way in which the past intrudes into the present. This reminiscence is enforced by the symbolic contrast between heat and coolness—the heat of the swamp and the city contrasted with the coolness of the sea and the sea winds.

Harboring the remembered pleasure of days when the "sarabande" of "wind" stirred in the "willows" and also of those times when "age had brought me to the sea," the poet faces with some regret the present swelter of his surroundings. He is in a swamp where "cypresses" tower in the hellish heat and where turtles rise through waters heavy with sediment ("sun-silt") toward the "sulphur dreams" of the sun. Just as the turtles fail to break surface and find themselves sliding back into the murk, so does the poet discover that he is momentarily unable to transcend the present.

The memories stirred by the poet's remembrances of the sea breed a nostalgia for the now no longer barterable experiences of "singular nestings in the hills" and the once-entered "pond" with its "singing willow rim."

At last the sea itself saves the poet from the futility of reminiscence, enabling him to pass beyond the oppressive memories of "alcoves," "gorge," and "city." The "alcoves" have been sweltering; the "gorge" is only an unrecoverable moment in the unrecoverable past. The "city" is pictured as a patient in need of anodynes ("scalding unguents spread") or as a victim of the torture of "smoking darts," and both of these images are suggestive of pain. To soothe these memories of torpor and pain comes the "monsoon" with its "wind flaking sapphire." Thus the final line of the poem thematically reverts to the poem's beginning. The "monsoon" in the poet's present world and the remembered sarabandes of the wind are both seen as reprieves sent from the sea. Caught in the net-like limbs of the willow, the "monsoon" brings to the poet a sound not of terror but of security ("steady sound").

"Passage" is related to "Repose of Rivers" both in imagery and tone. Like "Repose of Rivers," "Passage" is rooted in memory. It too offers an escape or passage from the sheer tyranny of remembering. Exhilarated as he was at the time by Slater Brown's invitation to spend a few days at his farm in Patterson, New York, Crane could not help but let his exhilaration creep into the poem. The tone of "Passage" is one of renascence, purification, "renewed infancy." Though he sulks in the poem, the poet is still capable of affirmation ("sanctioning the sun") and of responding to the promises of the wind before it ebbs and the smoke of distant mills is seen no more:

> "It is not long, it is not long;
> See where the red and black
> Vine-stanchioned valleys—": but the wind
> Died speaking through the ages that you know
> And hug, chimney-sooted heart of man!
>
> So was I turned about and back, much as your smoke
> Compiles a too well-known biography.

The poet then experiences a brief moment of freedom before confronting death ("thief") and becoming again aware of his inescapable involvement in time ("Sand troughed us in a glittering abyss") and also in evil ("serpent swam a vertex to the sun"). The poet then realizes that he will always remain a vassal of time. Trying to keep from forgetting the wind's promise of paradise and the distant sound of the sea beyond the "sapphire arenas of the hills," the poet finds that even the translation of a remembered moment into words will not endure for long:

> "Why are you back here—smiling an iron coffin?"
> "To argue with the laurel," I replied:
> "Am justified in transience, fleeing
> Under the constant wonder of your eyes—."
>
> He closed the book. And from the Ptolemies
> Sand troughed us in a glittering abyss.
> A serpent swam a vertex to the sun
> —On unpaced beaches leaned its tongue and drummed.
> What fountains did I hear? what icy speeches?
> Memory, committed to the page, had broke.

"Paraphrase" borders on prophecy after the poet has paused to explore the true and false notions of time. He states that the real movement of time is not measured by heartbeat, clockbeat, or the passing turns of a spoked wheel. These are simply conventional time-symbols which are related to the need of men to find some way to measure "time" even in its passing. But the real sense of time is something known only to one who wakes "at night" and finds "the record wedged in his soul." Such an awareness comes to the poet while he lies beneath "the clever sheets" that are draped over his naked toes. This sudden consciousness of the real sense of time has a fragmenting effect upon him. He finds himself thinking of the days that will follow his death and of the millenniums to come when his fossilized skull in some glacial dawn of the future will post a "white paraphrase" as the mute, single testament of his life.

> But from its bracket how can the tongue tell
> When systematic morn shall sometime flood
> The pillow—how desperate is the light
> That shall not rouse, how faint the crow's cavil
>
> As, when stunned in that antarctic blaze,
> Your head, unrocking to a pulse, already
> Hollowed by air, posts a white paraphrase
> Among bruised roses on the papered wall.

Even though the compression of "Paraphrase" tends to accentuate its difficulty, it is still a less difficult poem than either "Possessions" or "Recitative." Of these two poems Philip Horton has written that "even Crane was unable to give a rational explanation or paraphrase of what he had written." Of course, this is an untenable excuse for shelving critical discussion of the poems since the mere inability to give "a rational explanation or para-phrase," whether by the poet or anyone else, is in itself nothing against the poems as poems.

Crane's comment in *General Aims and Theories* is as good a guide as any to a consideration of "Possessions." Crane claimed that the poem "really cannot be technically explained" and added that it must "rely (even to a large extent with myself) on its organic impact on the imagination to successfully imply its meaning."

Reliance on the "organic impact" of a poem on a reader's imagination can easily lead to relativistic criticism, but it can be said with some safety that "Possessions" is essentially a contrast between life and the desired release of death. From "Bleecker Street" to the "smoked forking spires" of the proximate city, the poet turns with some expectation to the promise of the "piteous admissions" of his poetry. He recognizes that it is only his poetry that will record the "blind sum" of his "rage and partial appetites." Poetry will preserve this "sum" until the poet is finally possessed by death, which Crane regards not as an ultimate doom but as a Nietzschean consummation of life.

> The pure possession, the inclusive cloud
> Whose heart is fire shall come,—the white wind raze
> All but bright stones wherein our smiling plays.

The subject of "Recitative" is the dual nature of man. In this poem Crane sees man as a "Janus-faced" being with spiritual aspirations together with bestial inclinations. It is in the final four stanzas, beginning with a Darwinian allusion to the "ape's face," that the promise of the reconciliation of this duality into a single harmony emerges as a real possibility.

> Look steadily—how the wind feasts and spins
> The brain's disk shivered against lust. Then watch
> While darkness, like an ape's face, falls away,
> And gradually white buildings answer day.
>
> Let the same nameless gulf beleaguer us—
> Alike suspend us from atrocious sums
> Built floor by floor on shafts of steel that grant
> The plummet heart, like Absalom, no stream.
>
> The highest tower,—let her ribs palisade
> Wrenched gold of Nineveh;—yet leave the tower.
> The bridge swings over salvage, beyond wharves;
> A wind abides the ensign of your will . . .

> In alternating bells have you not heard
> All hours clapped dense into a single stride?
> Forgive me for an echo of these things,
> And let us walk through time with equal pride.

In these stanzas it is not difficult to detect certain foreshadow-ings of images that will be elaborated at more symbolic length in *The Bridge*—the office buildings, the skyscraper that holds the "gold of Nineveh," the spanning bridge itself, the stark and daily realities of "white buildings."

One of the finest testaments of Crane's ability to metamorphose images and themes through the symbolical and chromatic scales of sound and color is "The Wine Menagerie." This poem, like the others in this third category of lyrics, testifies to the formidable difficulties of analysis that such a transmutative quality of poetic expression places upon the critic. But the reward of such critical effort is the discovery that "The Wine Menagerie," apart from the three-part "For the Marriage of Faustus and Helen" and the six-part "Voyages," is one of the most perfect single poems in *White Buildings* and one of the best examples of Crane's mature style.

"The Wine Menagerie" has an unusual history. At a time when Crane was reduced to penury he submitted the poem for publica-tion to *The Dial*. Marianne Moore, who was then the managing editor of *The Dial*, agreed to buy and publish the poem only if Crane consented to certain revisions. Many of these revisions were entirely her own, but she insisted that they should be incor-porated into the poem. In addition to her decision that certain lines should be excised, she also told Crane that the title should be changed completely. In order to receive the small check that would keep him from complete destitution, Crane consented to the changes and deletions, but in a letter written in December of 1925 to Richard and Charlotte Rychtarik he could not conceal his bit-terness over what prompted him to accede to such editorial skul-duggery: "*The Dial* bought my 'Wine Menagerie' poem—but in-sisted (Marianne Moore did) on changing it around and cutting it up until you would not even recognize it. She even changed the title to 'Again.' What it all means now I can't make out, and I would never have consented to such an outrageous joke if I had not so desperately needed the twenty dollars."

"The Wine Menagerie" deals with the creative exaltation that Crane often felt when he was under the influence of alcohol. Philip Horton, relying on William James's discussion of alcohol in *Varieties of Religious Experience* as "the great exciter of the Yes function in man," explains that Crane's drinking "was not so much the cause of . . . revelations as it was a means to them—a liberator of immanent powers." The development of this very theme up to the beginning of the seventh stanza in "The Wine Menagerie" would seem to validate both James's and Horton's observations.

The poem begins with the poet's description of his ruminations in a rather ordinary saloon. It is there that wine "redeems the sight" even while the poet's eyes remain focused on the sight of mustard jars aligned like a scansion of so many poetic feet across a counter ("the mustard scansions of the eyes"). But his is not an empty reverie. Even in his near-stupor ("the slumbering gaze") the poet feels the "leopard" of his creative imagination, which is "ranging always in the brow," ready to impel him to assert a new "vision."

Only the "liquid cynosures" of wine are able to divert the poet from the images of himself that are reflected in the "bellies" of "glozening decanters." The repeated draughts of wine leave him "conscripted to their shadows' glow" while he pauses to observe a waitress framed in her passing against the background of a dado.

> Against the imitation onyx wainscoting
> (Painted emulsion of snow, eggs, yarn, coal, manure)
> Regard the forceps of the smile that takes her.
> Percussive sweat is spreading to his hair. Mallets,
> Her eyes, unmake an instant of the world . . .

The poet is suddenly impelled to shed his mortality as the "serpent" of the imagination sheds its skin in the renewal of original thought. After the skin of time is left behind, the new thought then moves like an "arrow through feathered skies." Anxious to preserve the creative moment that is being born within him, the poet ignores the unhappy reminders of mortality in the menagerie of the saloon.

> Sharp to the window-pane guile drags a face,
> And as the alcove of her jealousy recedes
> An urchin who has left the snow
> Nudges a cannister across the bar
> While August meadows somewhere clasp his brow.
>
> Each chamber, transept, coins some squint,
> Remorseless line, minting their separate wills—
> Poor streaked bodies wreathing up and out,
> Unwitting the stigma that each turn repeals;
> Between black tusks the roses shine!

At this point in the poem Crane is on the verge of a higher plane of consciousness. He is approaching a moment of almost mystical communion in which the poet strives to become united with the object of his vision. In reference to this moment in the poem, Horton has written that Crane seemed to feel that "in such identification there were tremendous reservoirs of spiritual power that once released would supply the elect with the pure, enduring stream of a clairvoyant vision which would be the distinguishing feature of a new order of consciousness."

Awaiting the release of this wine-inspired moment of creative energy are Crane's "new thresholds, new anatomies!" This leads to his awareness that the ecstasy induced by wine is capable of leading him into an empathic communion with others.

> Wine talons
> Build freedom up about me and distill
> This competence—to travel in a tear
> Sparkling alone, within another's will.
>
> Until my blood dreams a receptive smile
> Wherein new purities are snared; where chimes
> Before some flame of gaunt repose a shell
> Tolled once, perhaps, by every tongue in hell.

A significant comment by R. P. Blackmur relates the theme of this section of "The Wine Menagerie" to the broader theme of the transfigurative character of Crane's talent in the following way: "The principle of association resembles the notion of wine as escape, release, father of insight and seed of metamorphosis, which controls the poem; and in its turn, the notion of extra-logical, intoxicated metamorphosis of the senses controls and innervates Crane's whole sensibility." This statement, as far as it goes, is a valid comment upon Crane's method of working out his meaning in this and other poems in the third category of his lyrical output. Blackmur has supplied us also with the equally valuable observation on the idiom of this poem, which has already been quoted earlier in this chapter in a different context, stressing the linguistic problems Crane had to confront and solve in order to make the metamorphic experiences dealt with in "The Wine Menagerie" tangible to others:

> Crane habitually re-created his words from within, developing meaning to the point of idiom; and that habit is the constant and indubitable sign of talent. The meanings themselves are the idioms

45

and have a twist and life of their own. It is only by ourselves meditating on and *using* these idioms—it is only by emulation— that we can master them and accede to their life.

These passages from Blackmur's essay help us in understanding the way in which the theme of "The Wine Menagerie" is developed and resolved. The "escape" or "release" effected by the wine is doomed to be brief. Just as Keats wrestled to express his sense of desolation at the departure of the nightingale in his famous ode, so does Crane strive to forget his sense of short-lived ecstasy in the images of "sand" and "snow." The world of "sand" is the world of change, and "snow" suggests the perishable world of time. Both of these images are related to Crane's return to sobriety after the wine-induced moment of visionary insight.

> Ruddy, the tooth implicit of the world
> Has followed you. Though in the end you know
> And count some dim inheritance of sand,
> How much yet meets the treason of the snow.

Returning from the "feathered skies" of "freedom" and "new purities," the poet mentally stumbles over the relics of the inhabitants of his wine-visions. There is the head of Holofernes, the Old Testament champion beheaded by Judith; there is also the head of "Baptist John's," the New Testament precursor doomed by Salome. The two heads are described surrealistically conversing in mid-air in an image that links the Old and New Law. The poet himself is left like a run-down toy, a valentine of the Russian legendary folk character Petrushka, a pathetic animated cartoon of man himself:

> "—And fold your exile on your back again;
> Petrushka's valentine pivots on its pin."

Except for the two longer poems in *White Buildings*—"For the Marriage of Faustus and Helen" and "Voyages"—all of these shorter poems from "Legend" to "The Wine Menagerie" constitute Crane's initial lyrical moment. In their interrelationship these poems testify to his growing talent, his integration of the Symbolist and Imagist traditions into his own poetic style, his experimentation with the "pigment" and "texture" of language, his occasionally difficult but nonetheless meaningful poetic statements, and his willingness to innovate within the limits of conventional stanzaic and linear disciplines.

There are many who believe that the enduring value of Hart

Crane as a poet will be based upon his achievement in the best of these early lyrics. They contend that Crane exceeded his talents when he undertook to forge a type of American epic and that his fundamental romantic intensity bogged down in the sustained rigor of creating *The Bridge*. Important to a consideration of these claims, however, is the realization that Crane did not simply leap from the composition of shorter works to the composition of longer ones. "For the Marriage of Faustus and Helen" and "Voyages," as will be stated in the subsequent chapter, are particular cases in point. He proceeded mosaically in all of his poems, regardless of length, beginning with the splicing of image and image in the unifying and transfigurative moment of inspiration and working until he thought he had achieved an organic whole. As his conceptions increased in their scope, so often did his poems tend to increase in length. In many instances whole poems, which had been written initially as separate works, were grafted with other poems to form a single though more all-embracing work, as in "For the Marriage of Faustus and Helen," "Voyages," and some sections of *The Bridge*. But Crane's purpose was always the same. He strove to capture those realities that "plunge in silence by," to create his intricate "trophies of the sun," to shelter the "kitten" of poetry from "the fury of the street," to fulfill the promises of "new thresholds, new anatomies" through the Dionysian transfiguration of his own art.

3

◄§ KNOWLEDGE, BEAUTY AND THE SEA

IN CONSONANCE with Crane's "virtuosic" method of composition, "For the Marriage of Faustus and Helen" and "Voyages" were not composed in the form that they finally assumed in the Live-right edition of *White Buildings*. The three parts of "For the Marriage of Faustus and Helen" were not only written as separate poems but were submitted separately to various journals for publication, indicating that Crane himself thought of them as independent creations. Nevertheless, the three separately written parts of "For the Marriage of Faustus and Helen" do share a common theme that unites them. Similarly, the poems that constitute "Voyages" were initially six distinct lyric poems that Crane eventually orchestrated into a six-part study of the nature of love.

Regardless of their genesis, "For the Marriage of Faustus and Helen" and "Voyages" stand with "The Wine Menagerie," "At Melville's Tomb," "Praise for an Urn," and "Chaplinesque" at the apogee of Crane's lyrical achievement in *White Buildings*. They are the flower of his mature style and show him as a master of his own unique idiom.

FOR THE MARRIAGE OF FAUSTUS AND HELEN

The epigraph of "For the Marriage of Faustus and Helen" is taken from a passage of dialogue in Ben Jonson's *The Alchemist*.

The key to its meaning and the relation which this meaning has to the theme of the poem can be gleaned from the first three lines:

> *"And so we may arrive by Talmud skill*
> *And profane Greek to raise the building up*
> *Of Helen's house against the Ismaelite . . ."*

It is not difficult to show by a few transpositions that *"Talmud skill"* can be equated with Hebraism, and *"profane Greek"* with Hellenism. If *"Helen's house"* is suggestive of beauty, and the *"Ismaelite"* of Philistinism, it would seem logical to deduce that Jonson's meaning (and Crane's as well) is that the fusion of Hebraism and Hellenism—the two most fundamental cultural forces in Western civilization—is capable of defending and sustaining beauty against those Philistine forces that would destroy not only beauty but knowledge as well.

To carry on the implications of Jonson's passage into his own poem, Crane has implied in the poem's title that there is a possibility of an alliance or marriage between knowledge (Faustus) and beauty (Helen). The allusions to beauty in the poem are not only to the Helen of history and the symbolic Helen of legend but to a metamorphosed Helen, a girl riding in a streetcar, an abstract sense of beauty transcending personification. On the other hand, the character of Faustus is Crane—the speaker in the poem. Faustus has remained the accepted symbol of man's thirst for knowledge, and to Crane he was "the symbol of myself, the poetic or imaginative man of all times."

Before turning to a consideration of the body of the poem proper, it is interesting to note the prose statement sandwiched between the second and third stanzas of Part I:

> *There is a world dimensional for*
> *those untwisted by the love of things*
> *irreconcilable . . .*

This could easily be regarded as an addendum to the poem's Jonsonian epigraph as well as to the poem's dominant theme. It implies that there is no alternative possible for those sensitive to beauty except to attempt to resolve for themselves *"the love of things/irreconcilable."* Only those who are incapable of seeing anything beyond the *"world dimensional,"* which is the unimaginative world of routine duties, activities and observations, are left *"untwisted"* by the imperatives of love and, by inference, poetry.

Part I of "For the Marriage of Faustus and Helen" begins with

49

a description of the human mind reduced to the average in the *"dimensional"* world. Crane uses a eucharistic image to describe the "mass mind" as "the baked and labeled dough/Divided by accepted multitudes." It is subsequently described as inundated or otherwise muffled by such trivia as "memoranda, baseball scores,/The stenographic smiles and stock quotations."

The image of "smutty wings" at the end of the first stanza is transformed into "sparrow wings" in the second stanza. "Smutty wings" is suggestive of oppressiveness while "sparrow wings" suggests freedom or, at least, less encumbered flight. The implication of both images is that the mind, though inured to routine and though divided as so much "baked and labeled dough," is still capable of winging its way out of the oppressive world to freedom. It finds such freedom, as Crane suggests in stanza two, in sudden Platonic, intuitional ascents to an absolute world even when it is bound by "the stacked partitions of the day." Such freedom comes in sanctuary when the mind returns to itself and leaves behind the metropolitan hubbub and the world of buying and selling where the crowds mill and vie.

> Numbers, rebuffed by asphalt, crowd
> The margins of the day, accent the curbs,
> Convoying divers dawns on every corner
> To druggist, barber and tobacconist,
> Until the graduate opacities of evening
> Take them away as suddenly to somewhere
> Virginal perhaps, less fragmentary, cool.

At this stage in the poem's progress the poet becomes not only less objective and less concerned with the circumambience but also more personal in his attitude toward what confronts the eye. He finds himself "lost yet poised in traffic." He sees the eyes of Helen in a girl seated in a streetcar. The confrontation is casual and unplanned, but it prompts further speculations about the nature of the beautiful (Helen). Before his "arteries turn dark" in death the poet wishes that he might in some way be rescued by the spirit of Helen. He hopes that he might touch her hands somewhere, if only in the midst of the streetcar's "pink and green advertisements."

> I would have you meet this bartered blood.
> Imminent in his dream, none better knows
> The white wafer cheek of love, or offers words
> Lightly as moonlight on the eaves meets snow.

It could be taken as a phonetic fault in the last line of this section that the placing of "eaves" before "meets" complicates an already complicated grammatical construction. The assonance is unfunctional, and Crane's ear should have detected and eliminated it. But of more significance to the poem's theme is that the allusion to "dream" in this passage continues the running reference to Plato, which was introduced in the momentary and spontaneous flight to truth ("sparrow wings") in the second stanza.

What follows is an extended hymn to beauty (Helen) as revealed to the poet through the beauty of the earth itself. The imagery used is explicitly feminine: "limbs and belly," "throat and sides," and "bluet of your breasts." But it is simultaneously the "diaphanous" world of Plato.

> The earth may glide diaphanous to death;
> But if I lift my arms it is to bend
> To you who turned away once, Helen, knowing
> The press of troubled hands, too alternate
> With steel and soil to hold you endlessly.
> I meet you, therefore, in that eventual flame
> You found in final chains, no captive then—
> Beyond their million brittle, bloodshot eyes;
> White, through white cities passed on to assume
> That world which comes to each of us alone.

The poet then promises loyalty to beauty alone in the concluding stanza of Part I. With "a lone eye" fixed to the "plane" of beauty, the poet excludes all else from his attention. The image of the "lone eye" has been explained by Horton as Crane's "half-fanciful, half-serious notion that a certain intensity and clarity of expression in the right eye betokened a person of mystic predisposition or power." As used in this stanza, the image suggests a dedicated look into the private but timeless world of Helen herself—"to hourless days—/One inconspicuous, glowing orb of praise."

The second and central part of "For the Marriage of Faustus and Helen" is set in a penthouse night club of a metropolitan hotel. Whereas the spirit of Helen manifested itself to the poet in Part I through the eyes of a girl in a streetcar or through the beauty of the earth, in Part II the beauty of Helen, according to Horton, is revealed in contemporary versions of "the Dionysian revels of the court and her seduction" enacted on a "roof garden with a jazz orchestra."

Crane's attempts to capture the rhythms of jazz in the first eight lines of the poem have received more attention than the rhythm of the lines themselves actually justifies. It is possibly true that there is an echo of jazz tempi and syncopation here, but it is a faint echo. The only sharp realizations occur in the drumtap rhythm of line two and in the word "tremolo" in line three, which can be related to the vibrato trill of a clarinet or saxophone. Beyond this it is difficult to feel an implicit jazz rhythm in the prosody.

> Brazen hypnotics glitter here;
> Glee shifts from foot to foot,
> Magnetic to their tremolo.
> This crashing opéra bouffe.
> Blest excursion! this ricochet
> From roof to roof—
> Know, Olympians, we are breathless
> While nigger cupids scour the stars!

Against the background created by Crane's somewhat vague but certainly condensed onomatopoeia, the frequenters of Helen's twentieth-century court dance through "snarling hails of melody" until dawn ("somewhere a rooster banters"). Then they leave for "new amazements," descending drunkenly from penthouse to lobby.

The poet then moves out of the poem as a participant and becomes a commentator on the scene in which he had previously been involved. In Part I he had perceived beauty in a girl's eyes or in the beauty of the earth, and these revelations had helped him transcend for the moment the world of "memoranda, baseball scores,/The stenographic smiles and stock quotations." In Part II the poet contrasts two further aspects of contemporary beauty as they appear within the "metallic paradises" of the modern city. The first is the beauty of nature. Specified earlier as "the body of the world," this beauty is now revealed where "cuckoos clucked to finches/Above the deft catastrophes of drums." A second aspect is the deceptive beauty of artificiality. This is the man-made beauty of the night club itself. Under the "gyrating awnings" of the penthouse, modern man has attempted to create the world of Helen. But she is now no longer the desired Helen of Part I to whom the poet will lift his "troubled hands." She is instead a "divine grotesque" of the beauty of the earth, which was mentioned in the concluding lines of Part I and which was carried into Part II through the imagery of the "cuckoos" and "finches." Confronted by a "siren" rather than the regal Helen of Part I, the

poet cannot keep his disillusionment out of the final seven lines of
Part II:

> The siren of the springs of guilty song—
> Let us take her on the incandescent wax
> Striated with nuances, nervosities
> That we are heir to: she is still so young.
> We cannot frown upon her as she smiles,
> Dipping here in this cultivated storm
> Among slim skaters of the gardened skies.

If the poet sought the spirit of beauty (Helen) to save him from
the "stacked partitions of the day" in Part I and from "metallic
paradises" in Part II, he speaks from an even greater need in Part
III. He is no longer concerned with his own salvation from trivia
and artificiality, but with mankind's regeneration from the experience of war. Part III begins, therefore, with a uniquely modern
allusion to death as the "religious gunman" and proceeds to a description of the devastation wrought by World War I, which, as
Crane noted in his *General Aims and Theories,* is the modern
counterpart of the battle of Troy.

Speaking as "everyman" haunted by the presence of death
("delicate ambassador/Of intricate slain numbers that arise/In
whispers, naked of steel"), the poet seeks the regenerative catharsis of beauty even in the midst of war's destructive fury. The
essence of this section of the poem is a panegyric to the purifying
and redemptive effect of beauty upon man. The final effect of
beauty is not unlike that of the experience of classical tragedy;
beauty can "unbind our throats of fear and pity." It can triumph over war and flaunt this triumph even in the face of death.
Crane's language in this section verges toward rhetoric, but the
buoyancy of poetry never quite leaves it.

>   We even,
> Who drove speediest destruction
> In corymbulous formation of mechanics,—
> Who hurried the hill breezes, spouting malice
> Plangent over meadows, and looked down
> On rifts of torn and empty houses
> Like old women with teeth unjubilant
> That waited faintly, briefly and in vain:
>
> We know, eternal gunman, our flesh remembers
> The tensile boughs, the nimble blue plateaus,
> The mounted, yielding cities of the air!

> That saddled sky that shook down vertical
> Repeated play of fire—no hypogeum
>
> Of wave or rock was good against one hour.
> We did not ask for that, but have survived,
> And will persist to speak again before
> All stubble streets that have not curved
> To memory, or known the ominous lifted arm
> That lowers down the arc of Helen's brow
> To saturate with blessing and dismay.

The poet concludes with a continued insistence upon the need of our "conscript dust" for the "new and scattered wine" of beauty and knowledge. Militating against man's finding his fulfillment in the experiences of beauty and knowledge are the Philistine forces of the "eternal gunman" and the "brother-thief of time." Both of these images continue with variations the symbol of Philistinism suggested by Jonson's allusion to the "Ismaelite" in the poem's epigraph. But Crane the poet (Faustus) is able to turn on the deterrents of death and time and eventually to scorn them. Such deterrents are capable of defeating only those who are incapable of making or unwilling to make sacrifices for beauty's sake ("the shadow of gold hair"). The true lover of Helen is beyond such defeat.

> Laugh out the meager penance of their days
> Who dare not share with us the breath released,
> The substance drilled and spent beyond repair
> For golden, or the shadow of gold hair.

Redeemed and renewed by Helen, "the imaginative man of all times" (Faustus) is able to transcend the obstacles of time, war, and the other impediments of the Ismaelite. It is this redemption of Faustus by Helen that saves a suffering humanity and enables it to rise above the "meager penance" of its days. It is worthwhile to note here how Crane has transmuted several conventional Christian images to suggest the redemptive and sustaining effect of beauty upon man. The allusion to the "new and scattered wine" has an obvious Eucharistic significance. The image of "bleeding hands" in the final section of Part III suggests not only the crucified Christ but, by inference, a crucified humanity as well. Both of these allusions give additional strength and scope to the redemptive capabilities of beauty. Beauty is savior-like in its capacity to regenerate man and to help him transcend the "dimensional" world.

The thematic unity of Parts I, II, and III is stressed in the final lines of Part III. In Part I the poet pledged himself exclusively to Helen's "hourless days." In Part II he was momentarily diverted by the artificial beauty of a metropolitan night club and, swayed by music and drink, courted a "divine grotesque" of Helen. In Part III he experienced the catharsis of tragedy; the fury of war made him realize that the tyranny of the finite world could only be overcome by an imagination vitalized by beauty. This progression leads to the conclusion that Faustus must be united with Helen. Only such a marriage will permit man to prevail over war, to compensate for his failure to love, to safeguard him against compromise and deception.

> Distinctly praise the years, whose volatile
> Blamed bleeding hands extend and thresh the height
> The imagination spans beyond despair,
> Outpacing bargain, vocable and prayer.

VOYAGES

Philip Horton has cited two dominant influences upon Crane during the period when he composed "Voyages." The first was the influence of the poetry of an obscure poet named Samuel Greenberg, and the second was the homosexual excitation to poetic expression that originated from Crane's relationship with a sailor during the months when he lived in Columbia Heights.

Samuel Greenberg was a destitute, tubercular poet who died in 1916 at the age of twenty-three. Prior to his death he bequeathed his poems to an art critic named William Fisher who in turn showed them to Crane. Crane's admiration of the Greenberg poems was immediate and effusive. "Emblems of Conduct," which Crane included in *White Buildings* only at the insistence of Allen Tate, was almost a transcription of one of Greenberg's poems; Crane's reluctance to have it included in the book was undoubtedly because he felt it simply was not *his own* poem. But the Greenberg influence lingered. The extent of this influence has been adequately discussed by Horton and can now be corroborated by reference to the Greenberg manuscript recently published by New Directions. Horton says that

> When Crane read the (Greenberg) poems, he was completely beside himself with excitement. He stomped up and down . . . muttering the lines to himself and declaiming them aloud; he compared them to the work of Rimbaud and Laforgue. . . . It was an

important discovery, for the exotic visionary poetry with its curious entwined imagery of rainbow, sea, and flower exerted a distinctly traceable influence on Crane's "Voyages," which he composed during the same months that he was making transcriptions from the Greenberg Mss.

Whatever influence Crane's homosexual relationship with a particular sailor may have had upon the composition of "Voyages" is a point best left to psychological disquisition. There is nothing in the poems that explicitly betrays a perversion of the impulses of love, and there is no thematic reason that would lead a reader to relate the love imagery, where it does exist, to a source homosexual in nature. Consequently, a reasonable reader could find no compelling factors in the six parts of "Voyages" that would suggest that he consider the impulses of love in any but a heterosexual sense, regardless of the relationship that may have prompted them and regardless of the person to whom they may have been directed.

From a technical and semantic point of view "Voyages" stands as one of the most representative achievements of Crane in the third stage of his poetic development. Each of the six parts contributes mosaically to the poem's theme to justify Horton's observation that "Crane appears to have built up his poems in blocks of language which were cemented into coherent aesthetic form by the ductile stuff of complex associations, metaphors, sound, color and so forth."

The basic theme of "Voyages" grows from the concept of the poet as voyager. The sea upon which he voyages is the symbol of time, dissolution, flux, and nature. The drama of the poem derives from the fact that it is the destiny of the voyager to seek for love, and the self-knowledge that is the legacy of love, as long as he lives. Love, therefore, is capable of staying the poet even in the midst of the sea of time. The fact that the poet is still a creature of time and that the sea of time will eventually claim him is still unable to deter or absolve him from his quest. Such is the nature and the irony of all life.

The first poem in the six-part sequence is possibly the simplest to grasp. There is a more direct statement of the poetic point and less a reliance upon the "ductile stuff of complex associations." Yet, despite the relative simplicity of the lines, Crane does manage to infuse into them a hint of the deeper themes to come. The poem thus serves as a prelude to the remaining five poems.

Chronologically "Voyages I" preceded the composition of "Voyages VI" by four years, the latter having been completed in April of 1925. As was his custom, Crane resuscitated the poem when he realized that it would function as an appropriate preface or curtain raiser to the rest of the sequence. In a letter to Munson in 1922, he wrote: "It is a kind of poster,—in fact, you might name it 'Poster' if the idea hits you. There is nothing more profound in it than a 'stop, look and listen' sign. And it is the conception of the poem that makes me like the last line as I do— merely bold and unambitious like a skull & cross-bones insignia." Crane wrote this about the poem three years before it took its place in "Voyages," but the tone of "Voyages I" remained the same even in its new setting. It continued to be an omen and a talisman.

As the poem begins, Crane describes a group of boys ("bright striped urchins") as they play on a beach. They are unaware of the dangers of the proximate sea, and they frolic in a spirit of blithe unconcern. So long as they keep their distance, the sea will not harm them. Even in this first poem in the sequence there is a suggestion of the fatal power of the sea. It is not belabored, but the sense of death is present. Later Crane will let the sea come to symbolize dissolution of spirit and loss of personality. But in "Voyages I" there is only a mere hint of danger—a poster of what is to come. But it is important to note here that subsequent sea-symbolism in "Voyages" stems from this prefatory attribution.

The boys on the beach regard the sea from arm's length, as it were, and they remain oblivious to its power. It is the poet who omnisciently sees the whole picture. In his study of Crane, Brom Weber writes: "Do not be deceived, the poet would like to say. The sea is a mother, warm and maternal, which welcomes you to its bosom. But it is also treacherous—it has 'too wide a breast' to be satisfied with its love for you; you will be engulfed and destroyed in its embrace. Yet he knows that those who approach the sea innocently, as children do their mothers, will not heed his warning." Thus, the children emerge as prototypes of those who are unaware of the sounds of impending cataclysms until the storms actually break over and around them.

> And in answer to their treble interjections
> The sun beats lightning on the waves,
> The waves fold thunder on the sand.

The sense of warning becomes more and more explicit as the poem moves toward the portentous climax of the last line. The beach frolickers ("O brilliant kids") are told by the poet to enjoy their "shells and sticks" but to keep clear of those depths that could engulf and destroy them. The poet compares the children to a ship's rigging which the sea could crush in an instant.

The sea is then described as a woman for the first time in the poem and in the sequence. With "too wide a breast" the sea is loyal only to those organisms that live within it and draw their very life from it ("lichen-faithful"). But the sea is a deceptive lover; she is cruel to intruders and smothers them in her fatal "caresses."

> . . . but there is a line
> You must not cross nor ever trust beyond it
> Spry cordage of your bodies to caresses
> Too lichen-faithful from too wide a breast.
> The bottom of the sea is cruel.

In the total development of "Voyages," this prefatory poem serves two purposes. First, it equates the sea with death, doom, and dissolution. Second, it succeeds even as an overture piece in suggesting the sea's almost irresistible attractiveness. The subsequent poems in "Voyages" work out the implications of these two motifs, particularly in the continued personification of the sea as a woman. But if "Voyages I" stands as a warning to others, it is a warning that the poet himself does not heed. Thus M. L. Rosenthal is correct when he states that this first poem is "an overture in which the speaker advises his more childlike self (symbolized by the 'bright striped urchins' near the water) not to take the risks he knows he *will* take." [1] In "Voyages II" Crane crosses the line that he has warned the children and his "more childlike self" never to cross.

"Voyages II" is one of the most consummate fruitions of Crane's talent not only with regard to the other poems in the seascape sequence but in relation to all of his other poems as well. "The second of the *Voyages*," writes Yvor Winters in an essay not particularly noteworthy for its praise of Crane, "in fact, seems to me, as it seemed to others, one of the most powerful and one of the most nearly perfect poems of the past two hundred years." This is high praise indeed, but the poem justifies it. "Voyages II" resounds with the simultaneous release of all the dominant chords of Crane's versatility struck almost simultaneously. It is rife with symbolic personification, expert modulations of sound, transmutation and blending of some of the most beautiful imagery

[1] *The Modern Poets* (New York: Oxford, 1960).

ever written of the sea, the ebb and flow of simultaneously sustained and developed themes and a rhythmical progression that never loses its strength.

The impetus of the poem derives principally from an underlying sense of quest—a theme that is also at the core of *The Bridge*. The poet confronts the sea not only as a symbol of time and flux but also as a challenge to the voyager. But these confrontations are not separately introduced, nor are there the conventional transitions to aid us. The presentation is kaleidoscopic. William Van O'Connor has given a brief summary of Crane's indebtedness to the symbolist poets as they relate to the techniques used in this poem: "Like Mallarmé, Crane uses images which merge with one another and dissolve, only to recur in other forms or by implication. . . . Like Baudelaire, Crane suggests the unifying power of the mind by the use of synaesthetic meanings. . . . Like the more ironic Symbolists, he uses economy of phrase . . . and paradox." [2] All of these techniques are present in "Voyages II," and the serious reader must allow himself to become sensitive to them in order to keep his experience of the poem from becoming obscure or disturbingly cloying.

The sea, which is the poet's symbol of everything that is subject to death or change, is first contrasted with eternity. The sea is broad, but it is still finite. Even though the poet suggests the breadth of the sea by the use of such figures as "rimless floods" and "unfettered leewardings," he still can refer to it only as a "great wink of eternity."

After this introductory passage, Crane resumes the already mentioned personification of the sea as a woman. However, the personification is no longer anonymous. Crane uses the adjectival form of Undine, evoking the legend of the female water spirit who was promised mortality if she would marry a mortal and bear his child. This image testifies to the veracity of O'Connor's statement that "Crane uses images which merge with one another and dissolve, only to recur in other forms." Later, in "Voyages VI," Undine will be poetically metamorphosed into Aphrodite, indicating the range of Crane's willingness to lend to the sea different identities while keeping the female personification constant. The images are united not only by gender but also by the fact that something of the sea is common to both of them. Undine is a seanymph, and Aphrodite was created from sea-foam.

[2] *Sense and Sensibility in Modern Poetry* (Chicago: University of Chicago Press, 1948; New York: Barnes & Noble, University Paperback, 1963).

59

Exploiting the legend of Undine for his own purposes in the poem, Crane notes that the sea's "undinal vast belly" seems covered with a fabric interwoven with threads of gold. This is described as the "samite sheeted and processioned" surface of the ocean itself, its millions of waves reflecting the light of sun or moon. The transition from sea-surface to gold or silver fabric and from the sea to Undine is swift, and the reader is compelled to make the associations himself if he is to appreciate the relation of line to line, image to image, and word to word. The method followed by A. Alvarez in his explication of the poem is not unlike one that would have to be followed by any reader attuned to Crane's methods of composition in this poem. Speaking of the first stanza alone, Alvarez states that the

> action of the verse is difficult to plot; indeed, at first sight it seems to be made up only of a number of questionably connected phrases describing the sea. But seen from closer up it becomes clearer how the connections were made: how "wink" brought "rimless," which moved, with a jump, into "unfettered"; how there is a connection between the curve of the sea's eye and the curve of her "belly"; how "sheeted," "belly" and "love" interact, and how the "great wink" turns into "laughing."

If we follow Alvarez' critical direction, it becomes a relatively easy matter to accept the image of the sea—already personified as a woman—supinely "laughing the wrapt inflections of our love."

In the second stanza Crane introduces a musical motif to probe the mystery of the sea of time at yet another level. He imagines the sea as a harmony of melodies sounded in its tides. This harmony suggests not only the fear inspired by the sea but also the sea's (time's) power to include all finite things within its sway. It is here that Crane touches on the dominant theme of the entire sequence, which is that only those bound by the sacredness of love will somehow survive and possibly transcend the sea's (time's) power.

> Take this Sea, whose diapason knells
> On scrolls of silver snowy sentences,
> The sceptered terror of whose sessions rends
> As her demeanors motion well or ill,
> All but the pieties of lovers' hands.

The third stanza begins with an allusion to the mythical underwater carillons "off San Salvador." Horton has written that Crane "needed to hear only the bare outline of such legends as that of the sunken city off the island of San Salvador to be completely seized by a 'sea-change,' and to hear the tolling of water-muffled bells in the towers undersea." Inspired by the provocative mysteries of this legend, Crane introduces the first of a series of floral images into the poem. The stars become "crocus lustres" that bloom over the "poinsettia meadows" of the "tides" of the sea. The islands seem to dance to the sea's "diapason" until only the lover ("my Prodigal") is able to "complete the dark confessions her veins spell." Of subordinate but still germane interest here is the fact that Crane defended the sensation educed by the image of "adagios" as a touchstone of his poetic technique. His defense is worth quoting since it further clarifies what Blackmur meant when he wrote that Crane "re-created his words from within, developing meaning to the point of idiom." In his essay *General Aims and Theories*, Crane wrote "When . . . I speak of 'adagios of islands,' the reference is to a motion of a boat through islands clustered thickly, the rhythm of motion, etc. And it seems a much more direct and creative statement than any more logical employment of words such as 'coasting slowly through the islands,' besides ushering in a whole world of music."

The musical theme that is perpetuated from "diapason" to "adagios" is continued in the allusion to the sea's (Undine's) "turning shoulders." This image is particularly significant since it fuses the music of the sea with the image of the sea as a woman. Rhythmically she proceeds to "wind the hours." In an ironic image of proferring, empty hands, the poet remarks that the seemingly "rich palms" of the "undinal" sea are really "penniless." She does not give away her riches but keeps them to herself. What is given is only the world of "foam and wave," which is, in effect, the brief and finite legacy ("hasten, while they are true") of "sleep, death, desire." However, there is the possibility that the voyager can find the "floating flower" of beauty and love. It is because love is possible within the "rimless floods" of time that the last stanza of the poem becomes not a surrender but an invocation:

> Bind us in time, O Seasons clear, and awe.
> O minstrel galleons of Carib fire,
> Bequeath us to no earthly shore until
> Is answered in the vortex of our grave
> The seal's wide spindrift gaze toward paradise.

This concluding stanza is both an amen and an alleluia. The stanza begins with what is literally a request made of the sea ("O

61

Seasons clear") to suffuse the life of the voyager through time with a sense of wonder, mystery, and reverence. The poet desires that the "minstrel galleons of Carib fire" keep him adrift in the sea of time until his desires are fulfilled. The imagery in this line is fecund enough to continue the musical motif ("minstrel"), to evoke the keel-like and therefore ship-like procession of waves ("galleons"), and to reintroduce in the image of the Caribbean's surface flashing like flame under moonlight the earlier description of the "samite sheeted" body of Undine. The final three lines of the stanza are a further implementation of "Bind us in time, O Seasons clear, and awe." Spare us a shore-grave, the poet seems to be saying, until we have received an answer to the paradox that prompts us to look for some permanence in a life that is essentially impermanent. Our lives, like the sea, are subject to violent and continual change. It is love alone that can stabilize and save us.

Thematically the poem comes full circle with the reading of its final line: "The seal's wide spindrift gaze toward paradise." The instant of the sea-time image in the first stanza ("this great wink of eternity") is transformed in this last line into a "gaze toward paradise." This gaze is merely the outward manifestation of man's eternal search for permanence and peace in a life that seems to promise neither. It is, therefore, a perpetuation of man's sense of quest through time, where only the prodigal spirit of love can out-brave the "unfettered leewardings" and mocking laughter of the relentless years. Hence we are prepared to accept the poet's wish that he should come to know the staying power of love before he dies and that the hope of the symbolic "gaze toward paradise" is not frustrated.

"Voyages I" is a poster designed to warn us of the sea's (time's) treachery; "Voyages II" deals with the sea's terror, power, and seeming mastery; "Voyages III" presents the fulfillment of the poet's desire for what he both fears and loves. Despite the fact that the poet-voyager knows that the "bottom of the sea is cruel," he has in "Voyages II" chosen to become involved in the sea of time or change since it is the only setting possible for love. In brief, he has come to accept the fact that the experience of love can only happen within time. It is love only that can help the voyager avoid an "earthly shore." In "Voyages III" the conse-quences of this commitment are revealed.

Addressing the beloved at the beginning of "Voyages III," the poet acknowledges that the sea of time has a blood relationship ("consanguinity") with love. Moreover, he affirms that this relationship is "infinite." In an imagistic fusion of this "consanguinity" the poet likens the love "tendered" from the beloved both to the light reflected from the sea and to the sky that "every wave enthrones." Just as a swimmer turns aside the water with his strokes, so does the sea of time enshrine the relics of love with "reliquary hands." The implication of these lines is that time can be a friend to love as well as an enemy. In this sense the poet accepts the sea of time in the same spirit in which he acknowledged his need for love.

> And so, admitted through black swollen gates
> That must arrest all distance otherwise,—
> Past whirling pillars and lithe pediments,
> Light wrestling there incessantly with light,
> Star kissing star through wave on wave unto
> Your body rocking!

The immolation promised by love is then compared to death. But death in this context is not to be feared. It is "no carnage." Instead it is a love-death from which the new and transformed personality of the lover will emerge. Prompted by this promise of resurrection, the poet yields to the "silken skilled transmemberment of song" and addresses love directly: "Permit me voyage, love, into your hands . . ."

In this final line of "Voyages III" the poet praises and seeks love as the only victor over the more fatalistic themes evoked by his earlier allusions to the sea. His commitment is now clear and irrevocable. He would choose to voyage in love to preserve himself against the tides of flux and dissolution. Though involved necessarily in the sea of time, he would prefer to experience the sea-change of love rather than offer the "spry cordage" of his life to the "rimless floods," the "unfettered leewardings," and the "undinal vast belly" of the fatally attractive ocean of time.

This theme of fulfillment through love carries over into "Voyages IV." Love is first compared to a rainbow ("spectrum of the sea") that is able to "bridge" the limits of "mortality." The "counted smile" of love thus permits the poet to state that love somehow flows like a sea of its own between lover and beloved.

> Whose circles bridge, I know, (from palms to the severe
> Chilled albatross's white immutability)
> No stream of greater love advancing now
> Than, singing, this mortality alone
> Through clay aflow immortally to you.

Yet to achieve this immortal rapport, the poet admits that he must first lose himself in the "fatal tides" of what he called in "Voyages III" the "skilled transmemberment of song." In brief, he concedes that love must become and remain "incarnate" in order for its beauty to be known.

> In signature of the incarnate word
> The harbor shoulders to resign in mingling
> Mutual blood, transpiring as foreknown
> And widening noon within your breast for gathering
> All bright insinuations that my years have caught
> For islands where must lead inviolably
> Blue latitudes and levels of your eyes,—
>
> In this expectant, still exclaim receive
> The secret oar and petals of all love.

In "Voyages V" the rapture of fulfillment through love is interrupted by the demands of time as symbolized by the moon. Waking "past midnight in clear rime," the poet studies the horizon of "bay estuaries" and "hard sky." The cables that have held him suspended in sleep have suddenly been "swiftly filed," and he has awakened from a dream of love to find himself "overtaken" by "deaf moonlight."

> What words
> Can strangle this deaf moonlight? For we
>
> Are overtaken. Now no cry, no sword
> Can fasten or deflect this tidal wedge,
> Slow tyranny of moonlight, moonlight loved
> And changed . . .

Immediately following the poet's realization that love has been overtaken by time, there is a passage in which the poet vainly seeks to reconcile the world of love with the world of time. Love is symbolized by the touched hand of the beloved, and a "cleft of sky" replaces the moon as a time symbol.

> Knowing I cannot touch your hand and look
> Too, into that godless cleft of sky
> Where nothing turns but dead sands flashing.

The poet's attempt at a reconciliation of love and time is predoomed to failure. He is forced to concede that love is fundamentally at odds with time. In the final analysis love constantly seeks to deny or obviate days, months, and years. But here is where the thematic irony of the poem and of the entire sequence arises. Love is possible only within the finite world—a world of days, months, years, nearness, and distance. In such a setting it is capable of transcending the world of time. But man's nature remains a finite nature. Though he can transcend time, he still remains a creature subject to it. By eventually dominating man through the certainties of change and death, time is simultaneously capable of conquering love in a "flagless" and sudden "piracy."

In the poignant mood of disappointment resulting from this realization of time's ultimate supremacy over love, the poet urges the beloved to return to sleep. There he can dream of love and ignore, if only temporarily, the surrounding sea of time.

> But now
> Draw in your head, alone and too tall here.
> Your eyes already in the slant of drifting foam;
> Your breath sealed by the ghosts I do not know:
> Draw in your head and sleep the long way home.

There is something illusory and paradoxical about these last lines. They suggest an escape from the irrevocable realization described earlier in the poem. Clearly, time has triumphed. The moment of transcendence of love over time as expressed in the first four sections of "Voyages" has now come to an end. The lovers have been "overtaken," and, despite the temporary respite of sleep, they can never undo this realization. Henceforth they must remain within the shared sway of two opposed forces. Sleep is only a postponement. To realize their love they must continue to incarnate it through time and circumstances even though they know that time and circumstances are finally love's worst enemies.

In "Voyages VI" two dominant themes of the five preceding poems are fused and simultaneously suffused with the power of clairvoyance. The first of these two themes is that mortals are doomed to be engulfed by the sea of time and dissolution. But the second theme is that these same mortals are compelled by the paradoxical imperatives of life itself to seek love and its fulfillment while they still have time to do so.

As the poem begins, the time-tossed poet pictures himself as lost. He likens himself to a "derelict and blinded guest" driven on through "ice and bright dungeons," "ocean rivers," and the "harbor of the phœnix' breast." Though lost, he still cannot rid himself of his sense of quest; "blinded," he cannot find his way, and he compares himself to a "seer" in search of direction.

> Waiting, afire, what name, unspoke,
> I cannot claim: let thy waves rear
> More savage than the death of kings,
> Some splintered garland for the seer.

The poem then shifts its focus from the plight of the poet and becomes a meditation on the nature of creation itself. The mystery of creation, like love, is capable of revealing its secrets only through time. Time is here symbolized by another feminine personification of the sea—Aphrodite, the Greek goddess of love who was born of foam. According to M. L. Rosenthal, this meditation upon creation is the climax of "Voyages VI." "Speaking for all 'creation,'" Rosenthal writes, "he [Crane] insists that the 'blithe and petalled word' still holds its meaning for the goddess though it means ultimate destruction for man." Nevertheless, the poet is still drawn to seek what may destroy him. He desires some knowledge of the mystery of creation not only as the goal but as the very reason for his sea-quest. He admits that time will undoubtedly triumph over this knowledge just as it will triumph over love. But though he yields to the hard fact of inevitable defeat at the hands of time, he can still neither ignore nor abandon the need for the effort he must make to know and to love. The need to seek is inescapable. It is this sense of mission that gives meaning to man's life. He must always be in quest. The theme of quest in "Voyages" is actually the same theme that permeates *The Bridge*—the need to seek as something important and indispensable in itself, regardless of, and even despite, discovery. Edwin Honig has seen in this theme an echo of the artist's need to find in his knowledge and love of creation an answer to the mystery he senses in himself. It is entirely possible that Honig has suggested in the following brief comment the very theme that binds all six parts of "Voyages" into a single poem:

> The private place where the poetic vision re-discovers its source and from which it goes forth to do its work is associated with the sea in Crane's "Voyages." The visionary movement toward such a place and condition is not a retreat from reality; it is a journey to recover the buried heart of the poet's and race's identity, and to bring it back into reality. Here there can be no question of hedonism, willful obscurity, or romantic impasse; it is a matter of the simple necessity of the poetic imagination, which is to restore man's belief in his own image and self, in his own mortal continuity.

It is this spirit of "visionary movement" that is incarnated in the concluding stanza of "Voyages VI." Appropriately, this stanza is the conclusion of Crane's initial lyrical moment in *White Buildings,* but it is also a creed and a prophecy of things to come:

> The imaged Word, it is, that holds
> Hushed willows anchored in its glow.
> It is the unbetrayable reply
> Whose accent no farewell can know.

4

◆§ FAR ROCKAWAY TO
GOLDEN GATE

CRANE's search in *The Bridge* is a search for the real American
past and also for the lineaments in America's present that will
determine her future. *The Bridge* is appropriately divided into
two sections in which each of these aspects of quest is dramatized.
The first part of *The Bridge* from "Ave Maria" through "Cutty
Sark" presents the poet's westering search from "Far Rockaway
to Golden Gate" for landmarks of America's past, in the land itself as well as in cities, rivers, and ports. Going backward in time
as he goes westward in direction, the poet assumes the identities of
Columbus, Rip Van Winkle, railroad tramps, and derelict sailors
to equate his restless quest with seekers of the past and present.
The second part of *The Bridge* from "Cape Hatteras" to "Atlantis" dramatizes the poet's quest for a synthesis of the conflicting forces within America's present in an effort to create an apocalyptic vision of America's future. From this synopsis it can be
seen that the poet's quest in the first part of *The Bridge* is essentially a spatiotemporal one while his quest in the second part is a
spiritual one. Both, however, are realizations not of a historically
authentic America but of the real and mythic past as Crane envisioned it, not of the textbook America of the twenties but of an
America transformed in Crane's poetic imagination, not of the
clairvoyantly accurate America of the future but of an America

68

realized in the consciousness of the poet. *The Bridge,* therefore, is not a poem about an America common to all men; it is a vision of America unique to one man. Crane's America has significance in *The Bridge* as *a part* of his vision and not as something *apart* from it. *The Bridge* is primarily important as the testament of a poet and not as a chronicle.

Although the "Proem: To Brooklyn Bridge" prefigures the quest of the poet at the spatiotemporal level and the spiritual level, its principal value is that it forges the symbol that unites the two levels of reality. This symbol is the bridge itself, which joins the shores of the temporal world to the invisible shores of the spiritual just as the Brooklyn Bridge that Crane used as his model spanned the East River from Brooklyn to lower Manhattan.

The most important point to note about the bridge as the central symbol of Crane's poem is that it has a multidimensional meaning. In various letters to Waldo Frank, Crane tried to suggest that the bridge had much more than an architectural significance for him. This is validated in the poem itself where the bridge often loses its architectural identity entirely while still retaining its symbolic meaning. Crane was commenting on these very transfigurations when he wrote to Waldo Frank that the "bridge in becoming a ship, a world, a woman, a tremendous harp (as it does finally) seems to really have a career. I have attempted to induce the same feelings of elation, etc.—like being carried forward and upward simultaneously—both in imagery, rhythm and repetition that one experiences in walking across my beloved Brooklyn Bridge." Crane repeated these points in subsequent letters to Frank when he said that the "very idea of a bridge, of course, is a form peculiarly dependent on . . . spiritual convictions. It is an act of faith besides being a communication." In the blueprint of the poem which Crane submitted to his patron, Otto Kahn, he was alluding to no other symbol but the bridge when he used appositives such as "sweeping dithyramb" and a "symbol of consciousness spanning time and space."

These meanings of the bridge are important not only as a revelation of Crane's intentions; they are also all integral to *The Bridge* itself and indicate how equivocal were the meanings that Crane ascribed to his dominant symbol.

The bridge was essentially the meeting place of quest and transcendence, and from this fusion came the elation of "being carried forward and upward simultaneously." It is this sense of forward and upward movement that characterizes the various levels of the bridge's symbolism throughout the poem. The forward impetus suggests quest; the upward suggests transcendence.

Fundamentally, of course, the bridge was the real structure of cable and steel that the Roeblings had created—a triumph of human engineering and heroic effort over the Philistine forces that said such a construction could not be realized. Margaret Foster Le Clair writes:

> To understand even in part what Brooklyn Bridge meant to Hart Crane, we must travel backward through many springs to the 1870's when . . . Washington Roebling, paralyzed, his sight and hearing impaired, supervised the building of the bridge. He was the son of John Roebling, who designed the bridge and whose persistence over a decade had gradually convinced skeptical business men and incredulous state senators that a suspension bridge one mile and 709 feet long was not an impossible dream—that it was feasible to sink supports 75 feet deep in the sticky mud of the East River to bear a weight of 80,000 tons. We must remember, as his son must have remembered, the accident that took the life of John Roebling in the early days of the project. We must hear the screams of men permanently paralyzed as they returned to the normal air from the pressurized caissons in which they had to work under the river—among them Washington Roebling himself. We must see his wife, equipping herself with the necessary technological knowledge, become her husband's hands and feet. We must hear a disastrous explosion and watch the flame of a careless torch all but destroy the work of months. We must see a breaking cable lash 900 feet through the air to kill two men; we must watch eighteen others die during the thirteen years it took to translate John Roebling's dream into reality through the toil of many hands and the strength of will in a paralyzed body.[1]

This was to Crane what the bridge as bridge really meant. From this architectural or literal meaning arose the significance of the bridge as a symbol of human mastery over material by the combined force of vision and effort. The bridge, therefore, came to symbolize for Crane a triumph of human vision in shaping cable, cement, and steel for man's use. As ancient man left pyramids as his testament and as medieval man strove to realize his vision in the great Gothic cathedrals, so did the inventiveness of modern man make possible the construction of the Brooklyn Bridge in the twentieth century.

Ironically, some of Crane's critics limit the symbolism of the

---

[1] *Lectures on Some Modern Poets* (Pittsburgh: Carnegie Institute of Technology Press, 1955).

bridge to this level of meaning alone, which consequently converts the poem into a hymn to American industry. The transcendent aspect of the symbol is thereby stunted or destroyed. D. S. Savage, for example, bases much of his judgment of *The Bridge* as a "glorious" failure upon a somewhat isolated interpretation of the bridge as a vindication of American ingenuity. Savage's central thesis is that Crane's main effort in the poem is aimed at a sacramentalization of the spirit of modern industrialism: "What Crane was really trying to do, as a poet, was to give an inward, spiritual significance to the material, outward conditions of twentieth century industrial civilization. He wanted to take the whole complex structure of American mechanized society into his soul and to give it back again endowed with the spiritual significance and meaning of his own personality." [2]

It is true that there were some Shelleyan impulses in Crane that would lead even as perceptive a critic as Savage to such an interpretation of *The Bridge*. It is also true that Crane, under the influence of Waldo Frank and Gorham Munson, did come to believe that there was a possibility of effecting a reconciliation between man and the machine. It is equally true that Crane turned from a purely negative attitude toward the machine, which he described in an article in *The Double Dealer* as "the monster that is upon us all" and the destroyer of "the pride and pleasure of the craftsman in his work." But his positive attitude toward the "accomplished fact of mechanization" was not so much to sacramentalize it as to acclimatize himself to it. Crane formalized this attitude in an essay called *Modern Poetry* by claiming that "unless poetry can absorb the machine, *i.e., acclimatize* it as naturally and casually as trees, cattle, galleons, castles and all other human associations of the past, then poetry has failed of its full contemporary function." The key to Crane's attitude toward the machine and the spirit of industrialism that it stands for centers on the interpretation given to acclimatization. Does this mean a rhapsodizing of the machine? Or does it mean that the modern poet has the responsibility of utilizing such modern phenomena as "acetylene," "subways," "winch engines," and possibly a "bridge" in the imagery of his poems in the same spirit in which the poets of the past utilized "trees, cattle, galleons, castles and all other human associations" proper to the environment in which they found themselves? Additional evidence from *Modern Poetry* would indicate

[2] *The Personal Principle: Studies in Modern Poetry* (London: Routledge, 1944).

that the second meaning was the one that Crane had in mind. His position was that acclimatization

> does not infer any program of lyrical pandering to the taste of those obsessed by the importance of machinery; nor does it essentially involve even the specific mention of a single mechanical contrivance. It demands, however, along with the traditional qualifications of the poet, an extraordinary capacity for surrender, at least temporarily, to the sensations of urban life. This presupposes, of course, that the poet possesses sufficient spontaneity and gusto to convert his experience into positive terms. Machinery will tend to lose its sensational glamour and appear in its true subsidiary order in human life as use and continual poetic allusion subdue its novelty. For, contrary to general prejudice, the wonderment experienced in watching nose dives is of less immediate creative promise to poetry than the familiar gesture of a motorist in the modest act of shifting gears. I mean to say that mere romantic speculation on the power and beauty of machinery keeps it at a continual remove; it cannot act creatively in our lives until, like the unconscious nervous responses of our bodies, its connotations emanate from within—forming as spontaneous a terminology of poetic reference as the bucolic world of pasture, plow and barn.

To say, as Savage does, that Crane "allowed himself to be crucified" by the "heroic—and pathetic" task of putting a "positive and glowing spiritual content into Machinery" is unsubstantiated by the facts. This was not a part of Crane's aesthetic, nor did it reveal itself in the actual achievement of *The Bridge*.

In addition to the bridge's architectural meaning and its significance as a manifestation of man's timeless need to wrest the material world to his purposes, the bridge for Crane is symbolic of everything that joins or unifies. This is the third level of its symbolic meaning. Whether Crane is alluding to continents linked by sea lanes or years linked only by memory, it is the symbol of the bridge at this level of its meaning that is evoked.

Finally, the bridge symbolized Crane's reach for the Absolute. It was an emblem of man's reach from time into eternity. This final meaning of the bridge is apparent in such poems as the "Proem" and "Atlantis," among others. The transcendent aspect of the bridge is suggested here: the bridge as faith, hope, aspiration, the image of God's will as a "bow in the clouds." It is to this level of the bridge's meaning that Sister Bernetta Quinn refers when she notes that Crane's mind "reached out to Roebling's triumph of engineering as one way of expressing the means of union with His Creator, so passionately and blindly desired under all his excesses." [3] She also calls attention to Caroline Gordon Tate's tracing of the archetypal significance of the bridge as a symbol of faith in the *Dialogues* of Saint Catherine of Siena and other writers. Margaret Le Clair has added in her critique of the poem that the bridge "as representing unity and faith has a long and respectable history in poetry" and cites a few examples from a poem by Emily Dickinson as a typical instance of such usage.

◄§   §►

Each of these four levels of the bridge's symbolic meaning is evoked, however briefly, in "Proem: To Brooklyn Bridge." By incorporating these levels of meaning into this prefatory poem, Crane sounds the dominant chord that will be re-sounded with numerous variations in the body of *The Bridge* itself.

The "Proem" begins with the image of a sea gull glimpsed as it wheels above the girders of the bridge. To the poet the bird builds "Liberty" above the "chained bay waters"; in its "inviolate curve" it suggests freedom to all those who turn momentarily away from a "page of figures" to observe it. But the wings soon vanish ("apparitional as sails"), and "elevators drop" the office workers away from this moment of freedom and down again to the humdrum of the city.

The poet regards the city's people as "multitudes bent toward some flashing scene" of momentary release or distraction. The image is a clear reference to audiences watching a film that will continue to be shown over and over to other audiences. In the poet's use of "bent" there is even a note of anxiety or strain, as if the movie-goers were watching the film of their daily routines with more than usual interest. Again, as in Crane's "Legend," we are reminded of Plato's cave dwellers as they watch shadows of reality projected on a wall before them.

The poet then turns to the bridge itself "across the harbor." Forgotten are the apparently liberating curves described in the air by the harbor gulls, and forgotten also are the evanescent hints of freedom that the flight of the gulls suggested to the watching office workers. The poet strips everything else from his attention so that he may confront the majesty of the bridge without distraction.

> And Thee, across the harbor, silver-paced
> As though the sun took step of thee, yet left

[3] *The Metamorphic Tradition in Modern Poetry* (New Brunswick: Rutgers University Press, 1955).

> Some motion ever unspent in thy stride,—
> Implicitly thy freedom staying thee!

Here the poet is suggesting that the bridge has an imperative of motion even in its steadfastness; there is a freedom in its very stability. Perhaps it is this magnetism of the bridge's "liberty and permanence," to use Dembo's words, that lures one of the city's inhabitants to the bridge's "parapets." [4] Driven to near-madness by the city's pace and perhaps by his inability to orient himself to it, this "bedlamite" scales the cables in an apparent attempt to take his own life by leaping into the river. He teeters before the plunge, his "shirt ballooning" while the tension-breaking "jest falls from the speechless caravan" of those watching the bedlamite's desperate actions from below.

In another vignette the poet pictures the stifling noon heat of Wall Street where "the cloud-flown derricks turn" and contrasts this with the coolness of North Atlantic winds that the temporarily personified "cables" of the bridge seem to "breathe." The contrast of torpor and coolness speaks for itself, but it is thematically linked to the image of the "bedlamite" in the preceding stanza. For the "bedlamite" the bridge is a symbol of final retreat, a haven, an apparent springboard from misery. In the contrast between the bridge and the "street noon" of Wall Street, the bridge serves to point up the city's oppressiveness. Perhaps it was this oppressiveness that drove the "bedlamite" to seek the haven of the bridge. In this sense the vignettes are not episodic but conjunctive; one tends to fulfill and enforce the other.

Having regarded the bridge as a symbol of permanence, liberty, and vitality, Crane then raises the symbol to yet another dimension of meaning. This is the dimension of faith. The bridge, which in its "curveship" faintly echoes the symbol of a rainbow for the will of God, is transformed in this passage into a symbol of divinity itself. By ascribing divinity to the bridge, Crane may have overburdened his symbol. As a symbol of faith, the bridge has an archetypal justification. As a symbol of the object of faith, the bridge can be accepted only as an extension of the rainbow image of God's will. It is difficult to accept the plausibility of the bridge as a symbol of God in any other sense.

After describing the bridge as "obscure" as the promise of paradise, Crane ascribes to it the attributes of divine kingship. The divine king symbolized by the rainbow of the bridge is capable

---

[4] *Hart Crane's Sanskrit Charge: A Study of* The Bridge (Ithaca: Cornell University Press, 1960).

of rewarding and forgiving. These notions of reward and forgiveness embrace both the Old and New Testament. Reward or "guerdon" is related to the "heaven of the Jews," and "reprieve and pardon" are suggestive of the Christian tradition. In addition to its other levels of meaning in this stanza, the bridge has been subtly used to join or "bridge" the pre-Christian and Christian conceptions of divinity.

> And obscure as that heaven of the Jews,
> Thy guerdon . . . Accolade thou dost bestow
> Of anonymity time cannot raise:
> Vibrant reprieve and pardon thou dost show.

The spiritual significance of the bridge is then extended into the following stanzas. It becomes a joint symbol of aspiration and elevation or transcendence; it is the very fusion of praise ("harp") and sacrifice ("altar") eternally joined in a moment of inspiration or creative power ("fury"). Just as the bridge in Roebling's imagination was what carried the actual construction of the Brooklyn Bridge to its completion, so are all men capable of transforming the world of fact and transcending it with bridges of praise, sacrifice, and creative energy.

> (How could mere toil align thy choiring strings!)
> Terrific threshold of the prophet's pledge,
> Prayer of pariah, and the lover's cry,—

In the following stanza this symbol of the bridge as a unity of praise, sacrifice, and creative energy ("unfractioned idiom") is suddenly transformed into a personification of the bridge as a woman. It is the first indication that we have of the bridge considered in this way. In subsequent poems this symbol of the bridge as a woman will be particularized through the Virgin Mary, Pocahontas, a pioneer mother, and others. But the symbol in this stanza of the "Proem" refers to no particular woman by name unless the image of maternity invoked by "night lifted in thine arms" can be related to the Mother of God whom Columbus petitions in "Ave Maria." If so, the bridge's symbolism at this level would be strengthened since Mary has been traditionally revered as the mediatrix or bridge between God and man. There is nothing in the poem that tends to obviate such an interpretation. Moreover, this would help to justify the note of petition in the concluding stanzas and provide an appropriate transition to "Ave Maria."

> Under thy shadows by the piers I waited;
> Only in darkness is thy shadow clear.
> The City's fiery parcels all undone,
> Already snow submerges an iron year . . .
>
> O Sleepless as the river under thee,
> Vaulting the sea, the prairies' dreaming sod,
> Unto us lowliest sometime sweep, descend
> And of the curveship lend a myth to God.

These two final stanzas not only recapitulate much of the preceding imagery but suggest in miniature some of the themes that will be developed in subsequent poems. The allusion to the river, for example, is related to the long poem from "Powhatan's Daughter" entitled "The River," and the references to sea and prairie prepare for poems like "The Dance," "Indiana," and "Cutty Sark" in the same section. But these concluding stanzas also summarize what has already been stated in the "Proem." While the poet sees "in darkness" the true contour of the bridge as he waits "by the piers," he imagines that he sees an unbroken arc of power in its "sweep." This enduring "sweep" will outlast the transient arc of the gull mentioned in the first stanza. The bridge, like the gull, suggests freedom to the observer, but, unlike the gull whose wings were "apparitional as sails," the bridge combines liberty with permanence. The bridge also is capable of spanning "sea" and "sod." It testifies to the integrative power of human vision to transcend the world of fact. Finally, as a symbol of man's faith, the bridge suggests the human inclination to communicate with divinity—"lend a myth to God."

I

AVE MARIA

The opening poem of *The Bridge* is a soliloquy by Christopher Columbus. Traditionally, Columbus has been associated with quest and discovery. As such he not only introduces the theme of quest in *The Bridge,* but he symbolically incarnates in his real and archetypal identity the aspirations of the poet as searcher. Columbus is thus the first in a series of searchers chosen by Crane to symbolize his own sense of quest. This is in keeping with the basic argument of the first half of *The Bridge,* which is to explore the world of fact and myth in a poetic voyage backward in time to find the real American past. Crane must have seen in Columbus' indomitable desire to revise the traditional concepts of oceanic travel a counterpart of his own desire to rediscover America. In subsequent poems in the first half of *The Bridge* Crane will identify his quest with the quests of Maquokeeta in "The Dance," Larry in "Indiana," and the derelict sailor in "Cutty Sark." Crane has chosen his counterparts from different periods of America's past as he sees it, but the sense of quest is common to each of them and ultimately meaningful in terms of his own rediscovery of America.

Having studied as background material for "Ave Maria" such basic historical sources as Prescott's *Ferdinand and Isabella, The First Voyage of Columbus* and Whitman's "Passage to India" to which he reveals a spiritual indebtedness, Crane was able to fuse the Columbus of history with the Columbus of his poetic imagination. The fusion of these two strains into a single dramatic character is Crane's initial symbol of quest, pilgrimage, and man's search for the yet undiscovered. The Senecan epigraph (which may be translated: "There will come an age in the far-off years when Ocean shall unloose the bonds of things, when the whole broad earth shall be revealed, when Tiphys shall disclose new worlds and Thule not be the limit of the lands") not only serves as the prophecy that Columbus' discovery will fulfill, but it simultaneously testifies to the timeless desire of man to surmount old frontiers in his search for what lies beyond.

If Columbus is cast as Crane's first symbol of quest, the "Ave Maria" emerges as a further elaboration of some of the symbolic meanings of the bridge already introduced in the "Proem." The title of Columbus' soliloquy is not only a somewhat recondite variation of the name of the ship that brought Columbus to the new world, but it specifically identifies the Virgin Mary as the one to whom Columbus directs his thoughts. It may be, as Dembo has suggested, that "Mary to Columbus is more human and accessible than Christ," but it is also true that Mary is the traditional mediatrix between God and man. In this role she is involved in the symbolism of the bridge as a woman. Mary is thus the bridge or means of mediation between Columbus and the God whom he both invokes and fears.

The temporal setting of the poem is at dusk on the return crossing from America to Spain. Shortly before his arrival at the Spanish port from which he departed, Columbus becomes meditative and remembers the encouragement given him by one Luis de San Angel, an official in the court of Ferdinand and Isabella. Later in this first section Columbus acknowledges his indebtedness

to the Queen's confessor, Juan Perez. As he recalls the efforts of
both of these men in his behalf, Columbus rejoices in the fact that
he has justified their confidence in him and has vindicated his
original dream by the very success of his voyage.

> Be with me, Luis de San Angel, now—
> Witness before the tides can wrest away
> The word I bring, O you who reined my suit
> Into the Queen's great heart that doubtful day;
> For I have seen now what no perjured breath
> Of clown nor sage can riddle or gainsay;—
> To you, too, Juan Perez, whose counsel fear
> And greed adjourned,—I bring you back Cathay!

The allusion to Cathay is equivocal. Its first and most obvious
reference is to the land that Columbus thought he had discovered.
As is now well known, Columbus' purpose was to navigate to
Japan, India, or China (Cathay) in order to establish trade routes
and simultaneously prove that these countries could be reached via
the westward voyage from Spain. When Columbus was returning from what he thought was his discovery of Cathay and the Indies, he had no reason to believe that he had discovered the wrong
continent. Indeed, the American Indians are still identified by his
misnomer. Crane is simply being faithful to history when he has
Columbus say "I bring you back Cathay."

The second meaning of Cathay stems from Columbus' symbolic
role in *The Bridge*. It must be remembered that Columbus symbolizes man in search of the undiscovered. In this sense Cathay
is the land that all men seek. In letters to Waldo Frank and Otto
Kahn, Crane was quite careful to note that Cathay was "an attitude of spirit, rather than material conquest." He added that it
could easily be "transmuted into a symbol of consciousness, knowledge, spiritual unity."

While observing the sea from the deck of his ship, Columbus lets
the hypnotizing surge of the waters carry him back to the hemi-
sphere ("It is morning there—") of the land ("Indian emperies")
which he has discovered and left. This prompts further recollections of the hardships of the voyage westward from Spain.

> I thought of Genoa; and this truth, now proved,
> That made me exile in her streets, stood me
> More absolute than ever—biding the moon
> Till dawn should clear that dim frontier, first seen
> —The Chan's great continent. . . . Then faith, not fear

Nigh surged mc witless. . . . Hearing the surf near—
I, wonder-breathing, kept the watch,—saw
The first palm chevron the first lighted hill.

The disjointed sentences and phrases in this passage tend to capture Columbus' rapture as he neared his goal. As we read, we come to identify ourselves with him as he must have squinted westward to catch the first sight of the chevron-like silhouette of palm branches against the dawn. This suspenseful quality of the passage is heightened by ellipses and only slightly weakened by the somewhat pale compound "wonder-breathing."

There follows a second invocation of the Virgin Mary as Columbus recalls how the flagship, the *Santa Maria,* had to be abandoned on the journey. He then remembers how the record of the voyage had been locked in a barrel [5] and thrown overboard in case none should survive to tell others of the route.

Columbus continues to meditate upon the sea. He considers the sea as a world of itself between two worlds, a link between the old and the new, a bridge of water joining the hemispheres that are part of a world now proved to be one "turning rondure whole."

For here between two worlds, another, harsh,

This third, of water, tests the word; lo, here
Bewilderment and mutiny heap whelming
Laughter, and shadow cuts sleep from the heart
Almost as though the Moor's flung scimitar
Found more than flesh to fathom in its fall.

.   .   .   .

Series on series, infinite,—till eyes
Starved wide on blackened tides, accrete—enclose
This turning rondure whole, this crescent ring
Sun-cusped and zoned with modulated fire . . .

Columbus then relieves himself of an ominous prophecy. These remarks are not directed to the Virgin Mary, but to the Spanish king awaiting his return. Columbus suddenly warns Ferdinand against an avaricious ravishing of the new world in direct opposi-

---

[5] Crane's use of "casque" in his allusion to the barrel that contained the message has been the subject of some controversy, and Crane has been criticized for his use of the word. It should be stated that Crane may have been led to believe that "casque" (Spanish helmet) was an obsolete form of "cask" (barrel) ; both words derive from the same etymological source. Weber also points out that Crane spelled the word "cask" in an earlier manuscript of the poem and believes the change to "casque" was more likely an expression of Crane's "love of ornamental words."

tion to "thy God's, thy Virgin's charity!" He adds that the only fruit of such exploitation would be that Isaiah at the last judgment would find this new world denuded of its promise and its wealth.

> —Rush down the plenitude, and you shall see
> Isaiah counting famine on this lee!

Following this prophecy, the tone of the poem changes. As suddenly as he was moved to warn the king against imperialistic avarice, Columbus turns to the happier prospect of his approaching return to "Saltes Bar" and the port of Palos. His contemplation of the sea gradually becomes a contemplation of God. In fact, God is even identified with the sea to the extent that the sea tends to reflect to Columbus (and possibly to Crane) both God's power in its fury and God's peace in its calm. The sea is also a test of man's faith in the symbolic sense that man is a mariner who must voyage from the shore of birth to the shore of death on the sea of his God-given life. The sea is the bridge between the initial and terminal points of living. Columbus' attitude is that the true joy and challenge of living comes into existence not so much in the successful arrival as in the adventure of the crossing. It is not the port that satisfies; on the contrary, only "the sail is true."

> O Thou who sleepest on Thyself, apart
> Like ocean athwart lanes of death and birth,
> And all the eddying breath between dost search
> Cruelly with love thy parable of man,—
> Inquisitor! incognizable Word
> Of Eden and the enchained Sepulchre,
> Into thy steep savannahs, burning blue,
> Utter to loneliness the sail is true.

The subsequent sections praise the God of the Talmud who "grindest oar," who scans the "glistening seignories of Ganges" and the volcanic flame of Teneriffe and who alone is capable of bridging the "teeming span" of time and eternity. In the exaltation of this passage Columbus cowers before the power of the God of Isaiah to whom he has already alluded—"Elohim, still I hear thy sounding heel!" But this yielding to the God of vengeance and power is only momentary. Columbus crosses the Incarnational bridge from the Old to the New Testament with its promise of the now "unhooded" or revealed divine countenance. Manifest in the whirling "sapphire wheel" of planets and the "kindled crown" of stars above him, God's purposes become clear to Columbus. After admitting that there always must exist "one shore beyond desire," Columbus concludes his hymn to God through Mary with an alleluia that affirms the dazzling creative power of God—"Te Deum laudamus/O Thou Hand of Fire."

Even though the "Ave Maria" ends on a note of reverence and reconciliation, there is still evident in Columbus the aspiration to discover the "one shore beyond desire." Even death can beckon the discoverer. Thus *The Bridge* opens with a poem whose beginning and concluding images are interwoven with the basic theme of quest. In the broadest sense Columbus' quest not only parallels that of the poet; it is everyman's.

At the conclusion of "Ave Maria" the stage is set for the poems to come. The new world, whose rediscovery is Crane's object in *The Bridge,* has been found; Columbus has bridged the Atlantic from the Spanish to the American shores. But here a fundamental irony intrudes. In his discovery of the new world Columbus has brought with him not only the aspirations of the old world but also the original flaws of man that are as old as Eden itself. The future, therefore, can bring either glory or desolation, depending upon man's capacity for good or evil. It is with this in mind that Dembo's comment on the place of "Ave Maria" in the total structure of *The Bridge* assumes its most definitive meaning:

> "Ave Maria" presents all the elements of tragedy that the quest of the hero for Pocahontas contains. The discovery of an Indian Cathay becomes the narrator's discovery of Pocahontas in "The Dance"; Columbus' fear that chaos and indifference prevail in the universe becomes the narrator's fear that both he and his dream will be destroyed by an insensitive world; finally, Columbus' reaffirmation of faith in his vision of the sunset becomes the narrator's reaffirmation in his final vision of the Bridge. Columbus' voyage is both the epitome and the beginning of the Western tragedy. The arrival of the white man brings the ruin of Eden on the continent, but, paradoxically, it is precisely through men like Columbus—voyager and poet—that redemption is possible.

It remained for Crane to work out the ramifications of tragedy and redemption in the poems that followed the "Ave Maria."

II

POWHATAN'S DAUGHTER

The section called "Powhatan's Daughter" is the longest as well as the central one of the three sections that compose the first half of *The Bridge*. Powhatan's daughter, of course, is Pocahontas, and Pocahontas is Crane's symbol for the beauty of the American continent.

This central section of *The Bridge* is divided into five parts: "The Harbor Dawn," "Van Winkle," "The River," "The Dance," and "Indiana." Each of these poems is an examination of one area of the American continent or one phase of American history. In addition to perpetuating the spatiotemporal directions of *The Bridge*, "Powhatan's Daughter" is built upon what Sister Bernetta Quinn has called "a human replica of the Bridge." This "human replica" is Pocahontas herself, who continues the woman-bridge symbol already introduced in "Proem: To Brooklyn Bridge" and "Ave Maria."

In "Powhatan's Daughter" the poet becomes a twentieth-century Columbus. His journey westward from New York and backward in time from the present gives him the opportunity to discover for himself the body of Pocahontas. Sister Bernetta Quinn thus identifies him as Pocahontas' "modern lover." But unlike Columbus, who was voyaging to a strange land, this "modern lover" is returning to the "land of his origin and loyalties." While Columbus had the bridge of the sea to travel from the old world to the new, the poet is able to make his journey from the new to the old and from the present to the past only by means of the bridge of his own vision. And Bernice Slote writes that "In history, the complete realization of the body of America is through its exploration in space and time, and the narrative line is traced in the five sections of 'Powhatan's Daughter,' but with a fusion of present and past so that all of this happens in a simultaneous grasp of consciousness." [6]

"Harbor Dawn," the first of the five poems in this sequence, begins with no reference at all to the closing alleluias of Columbus' soliloquy. Its epigraph, which is a description of Pocahontas as a young girl, certainly cannot be regarded as a transitional device. We might ask: Is the transition not too abrupt? In "Ave Maria" Crane used Columbus to reveal the promise of the new world and at the same time to suggest its relation to the old. In "Harbor Dawn" Crane focuses on a scene removed by "400 hundred years and more" from the year of Columbus' discovery. Was Crane asking too much of his readers in expecting them to make such an imaginative leap without injuring the continuity of the poem?

[6] "Structure of Hart Crane's *The Bridge*," *University of Kansas City Review* (March, 1958).

Paradoxically, it is the very nature of the opening scene of "Harbor Dawn" that keeps the transition from "Ave Maria" to "Powhatan's Daughter" from being disturbingly abrupt. The poem begins with a description of the waking poet. Horton has perceptively called the poem's opening lines a dramatization of the "poet's consciousness" as it "wavers between sleep and waking, as though between past and present." In this halfway state between consciousness and subconsciousness or even unconsciousness, time is literally in abeyance. The waking poet has no sense of time at all, at least for the moment. This is the method Crane used to keep *The Bridge* free of, and in a sense above, the demands of conventional, chronological transitions.

In this state of semi-wakefulness the moment of Columbus' discovery of America is superimposed upon the present moment of the poet's waking in a Manhattan apartment. Using cinematographic techniques, Crane lets the past intrude upon the present and, with the same poetic license, allows the present to fade back into the past. This is true not only of parts of "Harbor Dawn" but of the other four poems in the sequence. This back-and-forth movement of time past and time present in the mind of the poet is proper to the symbolism of the bridge in the sense in which Crane defined it for Otto Kahn—"a symbol of consciousness spanning time and space."

In order to avoid a literal chronological progression, Crane chose as his subjects and symbols in the five poems of "Powhatan's Daughter" not the usual historical landmarks or figures but what he called "a more organic panorama, showing the continuous and living evidence of the past in the inmost vital substance of the present." The exciting experiments in movie-making during the twenties helped Crane to develop the means by which this "organic panorama" could be presented. The "flash back" technique, for example, is apparent in almost all of the five poems. It was not only convenient but common for artists to attempt to adapt cinematographic techniques to their art in such ways. The strides made in the motion picture industry during the twenties were revolutionary, and poets and writers could not help being aware of them. T. S. Eliot had shown Crane how such techniques could be adapted to literature in *The Wasteland*, and Crane and others had profited from the lesson.

Having begun "Harbor Dawn" on a note of semi-wakefulness, Crane evokes the sounds of harbor and city—"fog-insulated noises" of fog horns, a truck, winch engines, and a drunken stevedore. These sounds gradually insinuate themselves into the poet's waking consciousness. But they do not force him to become wide-awake. Ironically, the sounds that begin to rouse the poet are in themselves soporific. They actually succeed in leading him from one sleep into another. This latter sleep is not far removed from a reverie. In this reverie the sounds that were formerly grating become muffled ("soft sleeves of sound").

> The sky,
> Cool feathery fold, suspends, distills
> This wavering slumber. . . .

Still involved in his daydream, the poet becomes gradually aware of the woman sleeping by his side. While he contemplates her, she is slowly transformed in his mind into a counterpart of Pocahontas. In effect, this woman becomes the poet's bridge back to Pocahontas, and Pocahontas eventually becomes the symbol of the American earth. Thus is the progression of images established for the rest of the sequence. Pocahontas, who is a metamorphosis of Mary in the "Proem" and the "Ave Maria," continues the symbol of the bridge as a woman. She is also a symbol of America. Just as the woman in the Manhattan apartment receives the attentions of the poet, Pocahontas is destined to receive the attention and love of the poet when he finally discovers her.

> And you beside me, blessèd now while sirens
> Sing to us, stealthily weave us into day—
> Serenely now, before day claims our eyes
> Your cool arms murmurously about me lay.
>
> While myriad snowy hands are clustering at the panes—
>
> > *your hands within my hands are deeds;*
> > *my tongue upon your throat—singing*
> > *arms close; eyes wide, undoubtful*
> > > *dark*
> > > > *drink the dawn—*
> > *a forest shudders in your hair!*

Having thus forged the link between past and present through the Pocahontas-lover association, the poet reverts to the moment of his waking in Manhattan where the "window goes blond slowly" with the glare of the morning sun. The "cyclopean towers" of the office buildings appear; "window-eyes" reflect and "disk" the sun; a few "cold gulls" glide above the fog. It is in the final three lines of this concluding section of "Harbor Dawn" that the poet moves away from the description of a Manhattan dawn and gives "Pow-hatan's Daughter" its thematic direction. The "waking west" beckons the poet.

> Under the mistletoe of dreams, a star—
> As though to join us at some distant hill—
> Turns in the waking west and goes to sleep.

Just as the historical development of America was a westward realization of what was called its manifest destiny, so does Crane give "Powhatan's Daughter" westward impetus in the concluding image of "Harbor Dawn." The West that attracted the pioneers and fortune-seekers of the last half of the nineteenth century is revived and transformed as the goal of the modern poet-pioneer. "Harbor Dawn" is only a preface, an inkling, a summons. The poet has awakened to the sounds of the harbor and the city, but he is able through the medium of his female lover to heed the deeper reality of the West's imperative calling and of Pocahontas herself.

In "Van Winkle," the second of the five poems of "Powhatan's Daughter," it is Rip Van Winkle himself who becomes Crane's symbol of the bridge between present and past. Van Winkle is memory. Like Van Winkle returning from sleep to a changed time, the poet at the "same hour though a later day" remembers as he is about to leave for work a number of incidents in his childhood. Serving as frames for these reminiscences are the beginning and concluding stanzas. These give us a sense of the breadth of the American continent from New York to the Pacific coast—a bridge of land between two coasts. While the poet reminisces, he thinks of the "gun-grey" roads that lead westward, but he does not yield to their beckoning until he has first traveled the road back through memory to the time of his childhood.

> Macadam, gun-grey as the tunny's belt,
> Leaps from Far Rockaway to Golden Gate:
> Listen! the miles a hurdy-gurdy grinds
> Down gold arpeggios mile on mile unwinds.
>
> Times earlier, when you hurried off to school
> —It is the same hour though a later day—
> You walked with Pizarro in a copybook,
> And Cortez rode up, reining tautly in—
> Firmly as coffee grips the taste,—and away!

At this point the poet moves more resolutely down the road of memory. He remembers other historical characters encountered in early studies. He thinks of times when he stoned garter snakes. He recalls the "sabbatical, unconscious smile" of his mother. While he is involved in this reverie, the present yields more completely to the past. The poet's recollections, which are interrupted only by the intruding notes of the "grind-organ," gradually become more real to him than the workaday world of the present. As a result the poet succumbs more and more to the spell of the past and feels less and less inclined to pursue his usual routines in the present. It is then that the desire to travel West becomes irresistibly strong. Finally, the poet, the modern Van Winkle from a *"tenement/way down on Avenue A,"* decides that "it's getting late" and accepts the call of the westering road. As Columbus sailed for Cathay in the fifteenth century, so now does a twentieth-century searcher, prompted by a moment of introspection and self-discovery, become a traveler in quest of his own Cathay from "Far Rockaway to Golden Gate." Guided by memory, he begins this imaginative journey. As Philip Horton has written,

> Van Winkle served to begin the movement backward into the past again by accompanying the poet on his morning walk to the subway, the while his mind mingles recollections of his own childhood with the "childhood of the continental conquest" and its legendary figures—Cortes, Pizarro, Captain Smith and Priscilla Alden. By taking Rip Van Winkle as an indigenous genius of memory, Crane made him the "pathfinder of the journey into the past," a kind of Virgil to his poet's Dante.

"The River," the third poem in the sequence, advances the progress of "Powhatan's Daughter" and the poet's quest to the Mississippi River. Seizing upon the Mississippi with its wealth of literary and historical associations as the mid-country setting for this phase of the poet's pilgrimage, Crane had little difficulty converting the river into a deeper symbol—the river of time itself.

The poem opens with two stanzas of deliberately jumbled images. These stanzas have the effect of creating for the reader the kaleidoscopic view of the American countryside as it would be seen by a passenger on a speeding train. The train is called the Twentieth Century Limited, and this name readily suggests the tempo of America in the machine age. After the train speeds across the country—"whistling down the tracks/a headlight rushing with the sound,"—it leaves in its wake "three men, still hungry on the tracks." These three tramps are Crane's transitional symbols of quest. Having already identified the poet as a modern Columbus and Rip Van Winkle, Crane here sees in these pilgrim-pariahs or "ancient clown(s)" a prototype of his own sense of restlessness as well as of his poetic mission. As a result he uses them in "The River" as " 'psychological ponies' to carry the reader across the country."

After describing how the tramps watch the caboose lights of the Limited "wizen and converge" in the distance, Crane speculates further on the meanderings of such tramps as they wander back and forth across the United States where "Keen instruments, strung to a vast precision/Bind town to town and dream to ticking dream." He does not regard them as wastrels. On the contrary, he implies that these stumblebums, enjoying a certain freedom in their directionless journeying, are really more intimately involved in the life of America than those caught in the "vast precision" of towns and cities. The hobo, like the searching poet, is what Dembo has aptly called "time's truant." Each hobo measures time not by the clock but by the number of days required to travel, for example, through Ohio or Indiana. His is a world seen at a pace he himself sets. It is not the confused, tourist's world glimpsed willy-nilly through the windows of the Twentieth Century Limited—a series of disconnected progressions. The hobo knows the true meaning of time as it is revealed in the change of seasons, the cyclical flow of streams, or the rhythmic chant of songs. Like the nomadic Indians who roamed the continent, the wandering tramps know the rich secrets of the country because they are compelled to live close to it as best they can. They learn to adapt themselves to its contours, its changes, and its spirit.

> But some men take their liquor slow—and count
> —Though they'll confess no rosary nor clue—
> The river's minute by the far brook's year.
>
> .   .   .   .
>
> Time's rendings, time's blendings they construe
> As final reckonings of fire and snow;
> Strange bird-wit, like the elemental gist
> Of unwalled winds they offer, singing low
> *My Old Kentucky Home* and *Casey Jones*,
> *Some Sunny Day*.   I heard a road-gang chanting so.

Here Crane introduces into the poem an excerpt from a conversation among several tramps. As Crane recreates it, this conversation reveals a boyish naïveté together with an almost sentimental inclination to reminisce—"There's no place like Booneville though, Buddy." As the men chat, we come to realize that their goal in life is simply to seek the natural bounty of the land through itinerant adventures. They are true American gypsies, and the poet is drawn to remember how, as a boy, he was inclined to identify himself with these nomadic "ancient men" when he saw them behind his father's "cannery works."

> Hobo-trekkers that forever search
> An empire wilderness of freight and rails.
> Each seemed a child, like me, on a loose perch,
> Holding to childhood like some termless play.
> John, Jake or Charley, hopping the slow freight
> —Memphis to Tallahassee—riding the rods,
> Blind fists of nothing, humpty-dumpty clods.

Crane saves this vignette of memory from sentimentality by invoking the symbolic significance of the hobo's life. Because the hobo is involved in a "termless play" and because he stands apart from the "iron dealt cleavage" of the land, he touches "something like a key" to the mystery of America (Pocahontas). Thus the hobo and his counterpart, the poet, like the Indians who were their nomadic predecessors, are the true lovers of Pocahontas, seeking nothing from her but a knowledge of her "body under the wide rain." It remains for the poet to tell others of this knowledge. He speaks of echoes of the tribal past and realizes that in Pocahontas he has found a bridge through time and space that will take him farther back into the virginal wilderness of the continent. In passages like the following he lays the groundwork for the Dionysian rites of Maquokeeta in "The Dance."

> Papooses crying on the wind's long mane
> Screamed redskin dynasties that fled the brain,
> —Dead echoes. But I knew her body there,
> Time like a serpent down her shoulder, dark,
> And space, an eaglet's wing, laid on her hair.

The poet, having been precipitated into the past of his own and his country's youth, proceeds to contrast the land of the past with the same land at present. In a passage where poetic emphasis comes quite close to inopportune oratory, the poet speaks of the debt owed the "old gods of the rain" as recompense for the white man's ravishing of the continent. When Crane speaks of the "timber torn/By iron, iron—always the iron dealt cleavage," we cannot help being reminded of Columbus' apocalyptic warning in "Ave Maria." But the old gods "doze now, below axe and powder horn" while "pullman breakfasters" speed across the land from "tunnel into field." Beseechingly, the poet asks the passengers on the Twentieth Century Limited to "lean from the window" in order to discover the beautiful mystery of the land (Pocahontas) already and always known to the tramp-poet-Indian.

> Oh, lean from the window, if the train slows down,
> As though you touched hands with some ancient clown,
> —A little while gaze absently below
> And hum *Deep River* with them while they go.

In the poem's concluding stanzas the full significance of the river as a symbol of time is revealed. The river of time involves the hobo as well as "Sheriff, Brakeman and Authority." It flows eternally toward the gulf, bearing all humanity with it in its "one will—flow!"

> Down, down—born pioneers in time's despite,
> Grimed tributaries to an ancient flow—
> They win no frontier by their wayward plight,
> But drift in stillness, as from Jordan's brow.

The stanzas at this point become carefully rhymed quatrains. This tends to set them off from the rest of the poem. The effect is that the poem levels out, and the regularity of the meter and rhyme schemes suggests the unruffled flow of a river. The poet speaks of the "tideless spell" of this river of time constituted of the "alluvial march of days—/Nights turbid." The river flows over "De Soto's bones." But what the poet is really saying is that we are all implicated in this flow of nights and days, and only with patience will we reach the "biding place." In the final stanza the poet identifies the "biding place" as eternity. The metaphor is thus complete. The Mississippi of time flows forever into the "stinging sea" of the gulf of eternity. Having followed the time-and-eternity theme to its conclusion, the poet ends "The River," as he ended the "Ave Maria," on a note of praise, reverence, and resignation.

> Over De Soto's bones the freighted floors
> Throb past the City storied of three thrones.
> Down two more turns the Mississippi pours
> (Anon tall ironsides up from salt lagoons)
>
> And flows within itself, heaps itself free.
> All fades but one thin skyline 'round . . . Ahead
> No embrace opens but the stinging sea;
> The River lifts itself from its long bed,

Poised wholly on its dream, a mustard glow
Tortured with history, its one will—flow!
—The Passion spreads in wide tongues, choked and slow,
Meeting the Gulf, hosannas silently below.

The fourth poem in the sequence of "Powhatan's Daughter" is called "The Dance," and in it the poet is carried further back into America's past. As the poet strove through the symbols of Columbus, Van Winkle, and the hobos to discover the bedrock of the American past, so in "The Dance" does he strive to possess the world of Pocahontas by identifying himself with a tribal chief named Maquokeeta. In this poem more than in any other in the sequence, Pocahontas assumes the symbolic role that Crane destined for her when he defined her as "the mythological nature-symbol chosen to represent the physical body of the continent, or the soil. She here takes on much the same role as the traditional Hertha of ancient Teutonic mythology."

"The Dance" is one of Crane's most beautiful and yet one of his most difficult poems. Sections remain opaque even after the most careful and sympathetic explication. This difficulty can be attributed in part to Crane's customary techniques of rapid transitions, transfiguration of images, and symbolic associations. But in addition, there is Crane's mythmaking power to reckon with in "The Dance." Frequently in the poem Crane will identify himself with a figure without giving the reader the benefit of a simile or an appositive. The reader must accustom himself to this Shelleyan propensity before he can truly appreciate the poem.

"The Dance" begins with a meditation upon the Pocahontas of the past. She is pictured as having passed from spring to "autumn drouth," and her chieftain lover is no longer capable of resuscitating her. This Indian lover, like Pocahontas herself in her "autumn drouth," is part of the past and "holds the twilight's dim, perpetual throne."

The poet suddenly resolves to assume the role that the chieftain lover can no longer fill. He decides to leave "the village for dogwood"; he will return to the wilderness. By such a return he hopes to rediscover and revive the lost bride "whose brown lap was virgin May." He looks forward to a new rite of spring. The entire purpose of this quest, therefore, is that the modern poet may come to know the body of Pocahontas as "her kin, her chieftain lover" knew her. "Not only do I describe the conflict between the two races in this dance," Crane wrote to Otto Kahn, "I also become identified with the Indian and his world before it ['The

Dance'] is over, which is the only method possible of ever really possessing the Indian and his world as a cultural factor."

The description of the poet's quest for Pocahontas is unfolded in beautifully tooled and lyrical stanzas which are among the best in the poem. Having left the "village," the poet sails by night in a canoe to a rendezvous with the "glacier woman" in the pristine setting of the American wilderness.

> I took the portage climb, then chose
> A further valley-shed; I could not stop.
> Feet nozzled wat'ry webs of upper flows;
> One white veil gusted from the very top.

> O Appalachian Spring! I gained the ledge;
> Steep, inaccessible smile that eastward bends
> And northward reaches in that violet wedge
> Of Adirondacks!—wisped of azure wands,

> Over how many bluffs, tarns, streams I sped!
> —And knew myself within some boding shade:—
> Grey tepees tufting the blue knolls ahead,
> Smoke swirling through the yellow chestnut glade . . .

> A distant cloud, a thunder-bud—it grew,
> That blanket of the skies: the padded foot
> Within,—I heard it; 'til its rhythm drew,
> —Siphoned the black pool from the heart's hot root!

The imminence and circumambience of the storm and the thunder of the "padded foot" within the "thunder-bud" take complete possession of the poet and hurtle him backward into an earlier era when Indians roamed the continent. He seems to be an inhabitant of a different age, observing not storm winds over "birch" and "oak grove" but Maquokeeta, the "Sachem" or chief of a confederation, in a frenzied dance. When the storm of Maquokeeta's dance suddenly breaks in fury over the earth (Pocahontas), the poet is no longer able to remain an observer. He finds himself involved as a participant. Caught up in the spirit of the storm-dance, he identifies himself with Maquokeeta himself, seeking renewal in the Indian past. As the earth will be renewed by the rain, so will the poet be renewed in the echoes of the past evoked by Maquokeeta's dance:

> Dance, Maquokeeta! snake that lives before,
> That casts his pelt, and lives beyond! Sprout, horn!
> Spark, tooth! Medicine-man, relent, restore—
> Lie to us,—dance us back the tribal morn!

91

The image of the sprouting horn in this passage is an image of metamorphosis. Sister Bernetta Quinn has noted in this context how "antlers, like the sloughed-away snake skins, are . . . cast off as a sign of rejuvenation." Basing his aspirations for spiritual renewal in such images of transformation, the poet pleads nostalgically for a return to the "tribal morn" of the Indian and the country's past. To achieve such a return Crane seeks to identify his spirit with that of the dancing warrior. The identification is so complete that, in the subsequent binding and killing of Maquokeeta, the poet sees no difference between himself and the chieftain at the stake. In the martyrdom of the chieftain, the poet also dies. The dying Maquokeeta is a representative of Dionysus or possibly St. Sebastian; overtones of Dionysian sacrifice and Sebastian's martyrdom are both suggested in the stanza describing the death of Maquokeeta:

> And buzzard-circleted, screamed from the stake;
> I could not pick the arrows from my side.
> Wrapped in that fire, I saw more escorts wake—
> Flickering, sprint up the hill groins like a tide.

Death, however, is not the conclusion of the life of Maquokeeta. "Just as the drowned voyager [of 'Voyages III'] was 'transmembered' into song," writes Dembo, "so the burned Indian-poet is to be transmembered into the rhythm of the goddess-continent." This Dionysian transmemberment of the Indian-poet—"I saw thy change begun!"—has a redemptive effect upon Pocahontas. We must remember that Pocahontas in the first stanza of "The Dance" was described in the past tense—"She spouted arms; she rose with maize—to die." After the death of Maquokeeta, which results in the union of the Indian-poet and the "physical body of the continent or the soil," Pocahontas, the earth-goddess, is revivified.

> Thewed of the levin, thunder-shod and lean,
> Lo, through what infinite seasons dost thou gaze—
> Across what bivouacs of thin angered slain,
> And see'st thy bride immortal in the maize!
>
> Totem and fire-gall, slumbering pyramid—
> Though other calendars now stack the sky,
> Thy freedom is her largesse, Prince, and hid
> On paths thou knewest best to claim her by.
>
> High unto Labrador the sun strikes free
> Her speechless dream of snow, and stirred again,

> She is the torrent and the singing tree;
> And she is virgin to the last of men . . .

With Pocahontas redeemed by the Indian-poet, the possibility of reconciling the serpent of time with the eagle of space is assured. As the poet comes to know the real Pocahontas by repudiating the "iron dealt cleavage" and seeking only the virginal beauty of the land through identity with Maquokeeta, he bridges the distance between man and the soil. Moreover, this reconciliation makes possible other reconciliations of equal importance. "The separation of white and Indian culture is a corollary of the cleavage which has denied the natural and primitive reality and thus a spiritual wholeness," writes Bernice Slote. "But in a possible union of nature and man, best demonstrated in the cyclic, generative, fertility principle, time and eternity may also be reconciled, as well as time and space: 'The serpent with the eagle in the boughs.' "

> And when the caribou slant down for salt
> Do arrows thirst and leap? Do antlers shine
> Alert, star-triggered in the listening vault
> Of dusk?—And are her perfect brows to thine?
>
> We danced, O Brave, we danced beyond their farms,
> In cobalt desert closures made our vows . . .
> Now is the strong prayer folded in thine arms,
> The serpent with the eagle in the boughs.

With the problems of man-and-nature, time-and-eternity, and man-and-space apparently resolved at the conclusion of "The Dance," Crane would surely seem to have completed his quest for the real American past. As "The Dance" ends, the poet has traveled westward from the "village" and backward through time to find the peace of the Indian and make it his own. But this is not enough. The principal reason for the inadequacy of this solution is that the reconciliation of two such disparate cultures as the primitive and the modern is really not a permanent possibility for modern man. Despite the fact that the poet asked Maquokeeta to "dance us back our tribal morn," he prefaced this request by saying "lie to us." Apparently Crane recognized that the identification of himself with the tradition of the Sachem could not be achieved without some self-deception. The difference between the two cultures was too severe, and the time-gap itself militated against permanent union. The result of this impermanence is that the poet's quest, like the historical realization of the westering continent to the Pacific coast, is destined to continue.

"Indiana" is the next chapter in this quest. The woman-bridge symbol shared by Mary in "Ave Maria" and Pocahontas in "The Dance" is carried on in the speaker in this dramatic monologue. She is a pioneer mother, and her son, Larry, who is about to abandon the farm for a life at sea, represents the poet-Columbus-hobo type.

Despite the fact that the poem has been harshly criticized for its sentimentality by critics like Allen Tate and Hyatt Waggoner, among others, "Indiana" is nonetheless noteworthy as an appropriate epilogue to the other poems in "Powhatan's Daughter." It is true that Crane wrote the poem when the major work on *The Bridge* had been completed, and it is also true that "Indiana" is not distinguished by his usual virtuosity. But the poem, nevertheless, justifies its terminal position in the totality of "Powhatan's Daughter" by the very fact that it dramatizes the yielding of the civilization of the Indian to that of the pioneer. In "Indiana" the civilization of the Sachem lives on only in the image of a "homeless squaw" whom the pioneer mother recalls having once seen "bent westward, passing on a stumbling jade." The pioneer mother, remembering the spiritual rapport she felt with the squaw as their eyes met and "lit with love shine," becomes the bridge between the "redskin dynasties" mentioned in "The River" and the world of the seafarer that is to be the world of her departing son.

The pioneer mother and her husband, Jim, sought a Cathay in the West as did Columbus. Finding "God lavish" but "passing sly" in the gold-fields of Colorado, they discovered only the harsh nuggets of disappointment. With nothing to go back to in Kentucky, they left the boom towns and returned to settle in Indiana.

> A dream called Eldorado was his town,
>   It rose up shambling in the nuggets' wake,
> It had no charter but a promised crown
>   Of claims to stake.
>
> But we,—too late, too early, howsoever—
>   Won nothing out of fifty-nine—those years—
> But gilded promise, yielded to us never,
>   And barren tears . . .

The legacy of quest then passes on to their first-born son, Larry. Dissatisfied with life on an Indiana farm, he decides upon a life as a seaman. In the mother's last words to Larry as he departs, we have an explicit identification of him as the wanderer who perpetuates the sense of quest already symbolized by Columbus, Van Winkle, the hobo, and the Indian-poet:

> Come back to Indiana—not too late!
>   (Or will you be a ranger to the end?)
> Good-bye . . . Good-bye . . . oh, I shall always wait
>   You, Larry, traveller—
>   stranger,
>   son,
>   —my friend—

III
CUTTY SARK

The last of the first three sections of *The Bridge* is "Cutty Sark." This poem reveals a method of poetic narration that is entirely different from any other method used by Crane in *The Bridge*. Horton calls "Cutty Sark" a "derelict sailor's drunken fantasy of clipper ships in a waterfront dive, which was arranged as a fugue of two parts: the voice of the world of time and that of eternity." The "voice of the world . . . of eternity" is the tune on the pianola. The "voice of the world of time" is the voice of the sailor, who could well be an older and slightly more weathered version of the seafaring Larry in "Indiana." But regardless of his origins, the Bowery drunk in "Cutty Sark" continues the theme of the sea quest first introduced by Crane in the "Ave Maria" and thus concludes the first half of *The Bridge* on the same note on which it was begun.

The fugue between the voice of the sailor and the tune on the pianola symbolizes the two levels of meaning at which the dominant themes of *The Bridge* are developed—the level of time and that of eternity. "Cutty Sark," therefore, can be regarded as Crane's bridge between the first half of the poem and the second. The first half of *The Bridge* is concerned with the poet's quest in the physical and historical world; it begins with the voyage of Columbus and concludes with the spent wanderlust of a drunken sailor. The second half of *The Bridge,* as will be shown in the subsequent chapter, is more concerned with the relation of the world of time to the world of eternity and the spiritual predicament and destiny of man in the modern world. By introducing these two thematic levels of meaning as a fugue in "Cutty Sark," Crane was able to bring the first half of *The Bridge* to a harmonious close and simultaneously prepare the way for "Cape Hatteras" and the poems that follow it. It is not accidental that some of the images in "Cutty Sark" appear transformed in subsequent poems. In the transmutation of "Stamboul Rose" to "Atlantis Rose" in "Cutty Sark," for instance, there is definitely a preparatory allusion to the title of the final poem of *The Bridge*.

The title of the poem presents a slight difficulty. Cutty Sark is literally translated as "short shirt" and has this meaning, for example, in Robert Burns's "Tam o' Shanter." But Cutty Sark is also the name of a whisky, and we know that Crane had a preference for it from a remark made in a letter written to Caresse Crosby on September 17, 1929. Although the sailor and the poet are said to be drinking rum as they talk in "Cutty Sark," there is a tenuous connection between their drinking and the significance of the title of the poem. Upon final analysis, however, the title most probably refers to a particular British clippership.

Despite the impressionism of the fugue as Crane's principal narrative device in "Cutty Sark," the progress of the poem is quite simple. The poet meets a "man in South Street" and invites him into a waterfront dive for a drink. Becoming more and more garrulous as he grows more and more intoxicated, the old sailor begins to reminisce about whalehunting and the other trials of sea and land that he has survived.

> Murmurs of Leviathans he spoke,
> and rum was Plato in our heads . . .

If we keep in mind the Melvillian epigraph to "Cutty Sark" (*"O, the navies old and oaken,/O, the Temeraire no more!"*), we are somehow reminded of Melville's Ishmael. Like Ishmael or an updated version of Coleridge's ancient mariner, the rum-drinking sailor is prompted in his stupor to recollect his entire sea-life for his listener. He competes with the song from the pianola (eternity) as he tells of having to get back to his ship, of whaling in the "damned white Arctic," of abandoning the sea for a time to sell "kitchenware—beads" ashore, of the time he realized that his life, like the volcano called Popocatepetl, was a "geyser-beautiful," and, finally, of his resolve to return to the sea "—I can't live on land—!"

As the sailor rambles on, the poet thinks he sees the desire for further seafaring in the man's green eyes. Does the sailor still seek Cathay as Columbus did? Does he have the desire to discover far "frontiers" as the Indian-poet sought to discover Pocahontas or the pioneer, Eldorado? Or is this only the look of a man whose time is running out but who is impelled to sail the oceans of the world until death? The reader is left to his own conclusions.

> I saw the frontiers gleaming of his mind;
> or are there frontiers—running sands sometimes
> running sands—somewhere—sands running . . .
> Or they may start some white machine that sings.
> Then you may laugh and dance the axletree—
> steel—silver—kick the traces—and know—

> *ATLANTIS ROSE drums wreathe the rose,*
> *the star floats burning in a gulf of tears*
> *and sleep another thousand—*

With the voices of time (the sailor) and eternity (the pianola) still fresh in his mind, the poet leaves the tavern and crosses the Brooklyn Bridge on his way home. He imagines that he sees below him in the river a spectral fleet of clipperships. He cannot help but note that it was these ships (*"Thermopylæ, Black Prince, Flying Cloud"*) that actually completed the dream of Columbus to reach the real Cathay. Their captains traded for the "sweet opium" and "tea." They crossed the "green esplanades" of the Pacific and "ran their eastings down." But their achievement as well as the occasional loss of a ship at sea are for the poet only memories, and the beautiful names of the ships echo in the poet's imagination like the callings of never-to-be-united friends across great distances. Thus does the first half of *The Bridge* terminate. The quest through space and time ends not with certainty but with an echo and a question before the quest through the timeless, spaceless world of the spirit begins.

> Buntlines tusseling (91 days, 20 hours and anchored!)
>   *Rainbow, Leander*
> (last trip a tragedy)—where can you be
> *Nimbus?* and you rivals two—

>   a long tack keeping—
>   *Taeping?*
>   *Ariel?*

5

੩ THE BRIDGE OF FIRE

"CAPE HATTERAS," "Three Songs," "Quaker Hill," "The Tunnel," and "Atlantis" constitute the second half of *The Bridge*. If "Ave Maria," "Powhatan's Daughter," and "Cutty Sark" in the first section of *The Bridge* dramatized the poet's odyssey into the historical and mythic American past in order to create a synthesis that would reconcile and transcend the world of the "eagle" and the "serpent," the poems in the second section are more specifically concerned with relating that synthesis to the world of the present and the future.

Crane's principal concern in the last five poems of *The Bridge* is to examine the disruption of the continuity from the American past to the American present. His secondary purpose is to reveal how this discontinuity might affect the years after the "Years of the Modern." Each of the five poems, therefore, in the second half of *The Bridge* is meant to serve both as an exploration into one facet of this discontinuity in American culture and also as a prophetic affirmation of the poet's hope for the eventual regeneration of that culture. The source of this hope exists in the poet himself. Only the truth revealed in his poetic vision can show where the bridge between the past and present has been broken. Only the poet, says Crane in the concluding poems of *The Bridge*, can return our culture to its true course and sustain it there.

IV

CAPE HATTERAS

It is thematically apt that "Cape Hatteras" has as its epigraph two lines from Walt Whitman: *"The seas all crossed,/weathered the capes, the voyage done . . ."* If Crane's purpose in the second half of *The Bridge* is the Shelleyan one of revealing the poet as seer and source of society's regeneration, he could have chosen an epigraph from no more appropriate a literary progenitor than Whitman. Crane remembered that Whitman in *Democratic Vistas* and in his "Poetry Today in America" had similar conceptions of the role of the poet in American society.

Apart from serving the purpose of introducing Whitman as the person to whom the entire poem is addressed, the epigraph clearly suggests that the time of voyaging is past. The poet-seeker of the "Ave Maria," "Powhatan's Daughter," and "Cutty Sark" has returned home in "Cape Hatteras" to bring the wisdom gleaned from his quest to bear on the problems of today and tomorrow.

Basic to an understanding of "Cape Hatteras" is Crane's insistence in the poem that only the man of poetic imagination is capable of directing man's timeless impulse for discovery away from tragedy and toward truly human achievement. Modern man should never think that all scientific progressions are necessarily advances. If he ignores the visionary warnings of the poet, he may only be progressing toward his ultimate undoing. He should avail himself of the wisdom of Whitman, who is Crane's symbol in "Cape Hatteras" of the man of poetic imagination. According to Crane, we have not yet fulfilled what Whitman defined as America's promise. Therefore, someone in this century must resuscitate Whitman's vision. In the epigraph to "Cape Hatteras" as well as in the final lines of the poem, Crane seeks to accomplish this by allying his own talent and vision with Whitman's in order to bridge the years that divide the two men.

Whitman was to Crane what Virgil was to Dante. The question of Whitman's reliability as the best prophet and guide that Crane could have chosen is in a sense irrelevant here. The fact remains that Crane believed that Whitman could fulfill these roles and that such roles were capable of fulfillment only by a man of poetic imagination. To say, as William Van O'Connor has said, that "Crane was caught up by the shallow optimism, a part of the Whitman vogue which, for a number of reasons, carried many of his generation downstream" is really of only questionable value to any final estimate of the success or failure of "Cape Hatteras." Such an opinion, though interesting as literary history, is based upon a personal estimate of Whitman's significance in American letters and not upon the depiction of Whitman in Crane's poem. Whitman's significance in the poem is directly proportional to the significance he had for Hart Crane, and the tone of "Cape Hatteras" merely reflects the spirit of admiration that Crane had for Whitman as revealed in a letter which Crane wrote to Allen Tate on July 13, 1930:

> But since you and I hold such divergent prejudices regarding the value of the materials and events that W. [Whitman] responded to, and especially as you, like so many others, never seem to have read his *Democratic Vistas* and other of his statements sharply decrying the materialism, industrialism, etc., of which you name him the guilty and hysterical spokesman, there isn't much use in my tabulating the qualified, yet persistent reasons I have for my admiration of him, and my allegiance to the positive and universal tendencies implicit in nearly all his best work.

More in keeping with the spirit that animated Crane in "Cape Hatteras" is the prefatory comment of Bernice Slote to her brief but perceptive examination of the poem: "To think of the structure of 'Cape Hatteras' as showing, first, the human condition; second, the human failure; and third, the rise to infinity through the way set down by Whitman, will give it a consistent form. As a miscellaneous praise of geology, or science, or of Whitman, it will be a fumbling, sentimental effort."

The bridging symbols between "Cutty Sark" and "Cape Hatteras" are both the sea and the seafarer. In "Cutty Sark" the derelict sailor was last seen stumbling down the Bowery toward his ship and in all probability toward the "frontiers gleaming of his mind." In "Cape Hatteras" the poet-voyager has returned to the shore.

As the poem begins, the poet sees the cape as a huge sea beast disappearing "mammoth" and lizard-like at the eastern horizon. Remembering the "strange tongues" heard on his travels, the "songs that gypsies dealt us at Marseille," the priests who "walked —slowly through Bombay," the poet ruminates before his own hearth. But he has no desire to take to the sea again. Instead he will remain ashore "in thrall" to the "deep wonderment" of the beauty of the land—"red, eternal flesh of Pocahontas." He is convinced that this "wonderment" still exists "surcharged/With sweetness below derricks, chimneys, tunnels" but is suddenly jolted from this speculation by a moment of clairvoyance in which he has intimations of the achievement and tragedy of the years to come:

> . . . time clears
> Our lenses, lifts a focus, resurrects
> A periscope to glimpse what joys or pain
> Our eyes can share or answer—then deflects
> Us, shunting to a labyrinth submersed
> Where each sees only his dim past reversed . . .

After this preface comes the first of the poem's two major sections. The first section deals with man's conquest of space through the science of aeronautics and the tragedy of such achievement when turned to destructive purposes. The second section deals with the direction that the poetic vision can give to man's technical achievement to save it from tragedy.

As the sea in "Voyages II" was for Crane a "great wink of eternity," so does the sky become for him a "star-glistered salver of infinity" in "Cape Hatteras." Like the sea, the sky has the capability to attract us; it "consumes us in its smile." Within the "blind crucibles of endless space" modern man seeks the same answers and discoveries that Adam sought but with different means. The era of modern man is one when "the eagle dominates our days."

After a somewhat lusterless progression of rhymed pentameters, Crane invokes the name of Walt Whitman for the first time. Comparing Whitman's vision with that of Columbus in "Ave Maria" ("like the Great Navigator's without ship"), Crane claims that the true achievement of America predicted by Whitman has not been realized in our time despite the inventiveness that has enabled man to conquer the sky. In other words, the fulfillment of Whitman's dream is still to come. For this reason Crane can describe Whitman as the "saunterer on free ways still ahead" and claim that the world of "canyoned traffic," "stocks," and "abandoned pastures" is not "our empire yet."

Crane then scrutinizes man's advances in aeronautics. He acknowledges that the "nasal whine of power whips a new universe." He concedes that the "gigantic power house" of "dynamos" is now "wound, bobbin-bound, refined." But he follows these concessions with a question—"Towards what?" Instead of receiving an answer, the poet's question is drowned by the "split thunder" of a plane's "whirling armatures." In brief, the answer of the machine age to the poet's question is the blare of an engine. Having ignored and silenced the poet's voice, the "blind ecstasy" of the skyfarer is without direction. As a result, the achievement of "the Wright windwrestlers" at Kitty Hawk is capable of being easily adapted to destruction. The airplane is thus transformed into an instrument of war ("knows the closer clasp of Mars") and gain ("fierce schedules, rife of doom apace"). Designed for destruction or profit rather than exploration, the warplane is described as part of a "dragon's covey."

> While Iliads glimmer through eyes raised in pride
> Hell's belt springs wider into heaven's plumed side.
> O bright circumferences, heights employed to fly
> War's fiery kennel masked in downy offings,—
> This tournament of space, the threshed and chiselled height,
> Is baited by marauding circles, bludgeon flail
> Of rancorous grenades whose screaming petals carve us
> Wounds that we wrap with theorems sharp as hail!

Crane particularizes the military aspect of man's conquest of space with a description of planes being wheeled "from larval-silver hangars" before they veer to "shear Cumulus" while "convoy planes" circle the "Cetus-like" dirigible. Despite the range and occasional brilliance of imagery in this passage, the language is often turgid without a corresponding justification for turgidity in the subject. The tone of the lines is more rhapsodic than poetic.

The poet then draws closer and closer to the aviator himself. This aviator, the Columbus of space, is faced by the prospect of becoming only a force for destructiveness. The poet, therefore, reminds him that it is his duty, as it is the poet's, to reach for those perfections that will contribute to the good of man. The aviator is urged to supplant a destructive goal with a constructive one.

> Thine eyes bicarbonated white by speed, O Skygak, see
> How from thy path above the levin's lance
> Thou sowest doom thou hast nor time nor chance
> To reckon—as thy stilly eyes partake
> What alcohol of space . . . ! Remember, Falcon-Ace,
> Thou hast there in thy wrist a Sanskrit charge
> To conjugate infinity's dim marge—
> Anew . . . !

Unfortunately, the aviator must first experience the tragedy that is the inevitable result of his unguided conquest of the sky before he can become possessed of poetic wisdom. Crane dramatizes this tragedy in a description of the crash of an airplane. Like Icarus, modern man's tragic flaw is that he has let himself become

the victim of his own inventiveness. But his tragedy may be a
"reprieve" if he is willing to purge himself of his *hybris* of scien-
tism and direct machinery to a more positive purpose than war.

> But first, here at this height receive
> The benediction of the shell's deep, sure reprieve!
> Lead-perforated fuselage, escutcheoned wings
> Lift agonized quittance, tilting from the invisible brink
> Now eagle-bright, now
>   quarry-hid, twist-
>   -ing, sink with
> Enormous repercussive list-
>   -ings down
> Giddily spiralled
>   gauntlets, upturned, unlooping
> In guerrilla sleights, trapped in combustion gyr-
> Ing, dance the curdled depth
>   down whizzing
> Zodiacs, dashed
>   (now nearing fast the Cape!)
>   down gravitation's
>   vortex into crashed
> . . . dispersion . . . into mashed and shapeless débris. . . .
> By Hatteras bunched the beached heap of high bravery!

The Icarian crash of the airplane concludes the first section of
the poem. The second section is concerned with the seemingly en-
lightened and regenerated world that needed the catharsis of the
crash to bring it into being. "Like the high-flying soul, modern
man, the Falcon-Ace," writes Dembo, "is led on by infinity; because he is blind, he will kill himself, but will rise again to achieve
a true insight or carry out the Sanskrit charge that beats in his
pulse." Phoenix-like out of the ashes of the crashed plane rises
Crane's invocation of Whitman. Whitman, according to Crane,
has shown himself aware of man's "deepest soundings." Because
he has observed the waste of war and known the tragedy of "fra-
ternal massacre" during the Civil War, Whitman is chosen by
Crane to lead modern man out of the "blind ecstasy" whose ultimate end is disaster.

> Thou, pallid there as chalk,
> Hast kept of wounds, O Mourner, all that sum
> That then from Appomattox stretched to Somme!

Crane then proceeds to apostrophize Whitman, as James E. Miller, Jr., has noted, not as the "conventional yawping American

chauvinist" but as "a maker of a complex myth of possible future fulfillment." [1] In this spirit Crane regards Whitman as a co-builder of the bridge that is his poem's dominant symbol.

> Our Meistersinger, thou set breath in steel;
> And it was thou who on the boldest heel
> Stood up and flung the span on even wing
> Of that great Bridge, our Myth, whereof I sing!

Crane not only acknowledges his debt to Whitman as a co-creator of this bridge of faith, vision and hope, but he goes on to identify Whitman's vision as an almost Messianic answer to the need of modern man to find a way out of tragedy in order to fulfill his own and America's national promise. Crane, therefore, refers to Whitman as *"Panis Angelicus,"* and this sacramental image is coherent despite Horton's claim that Crane was "under the impression that he was hailing him [Whitman] as Holy Pan." Whitman, according to Crane, is destined to be a Eucharistic part of modern man as he is also destined to be a "Vedic Caesar" whose vision will be capable of exceeding and directing all "sesames of science." When modern man accepts the spiritual legacy of Whitman, even the flight of planes will be redeemed and transformed by the poetic imagination into "Easters of speeding light."

As the poem concludes, Crane repeats the image of the dinosaurian cape that he used at the poem's beginning. But it is now spanned by the "rainbow's arch," which is a recognizable variation of the bridge image as a triumphant symbol of the poetic "consciousness spanning time and space." Thus the poem ends, as Waggoner has said, with "Crane dedicating himself and his poem to Whitman's kind of transcendentalism, a mysticism 'inclusive' of science and the machine, yet also both fundamentally and ultimately intuitive." [2]

> Yes, Walt,
> Afoot again, and onward without halt,—
> Not soon, nor suddenly,—No, never to let go
> My hand
> in yours,
> Walt Whitman—
> so—

[1] *Start with the Sun* (Lincoln: University of Nebraska Press. 1960).
[2] *The Heel of Elohim: Science and Values in Modern Poetry* (Norman: University of Oklahoma Press, 1950).

V

THREE SONGS

The section called "Three Songs," though it has been criticized by Winters, Weber, and Waggoner as having no thematic justification for being included in the second half of *The Bridge*, is organically related to the symbol of the bridge as a woman. The Virgin Mary, Pocahontas, and a pioneer mother sustained this dimension of the bridge's meaning in the first half of the poem. In the second half of the poem the triptych of "Three Songs" dramatizes the breakdown of the Pocahontas symbol in the modern world. Pocahontas is no longer the beautiful lover known in "Harbor Dawn," nor is she the "glacier woman" pursued in "The Dance." She is now a woman who inveigles but does not satisfy, and Crane thus personifies her as a prostitute in "Southern Cross," a strip-teaser in "National Winter Garden," and a seemingly demure secretary in "Virginia."

In the first song, "Southern Cross," the stars of the Southern Cross constellation suggest Pocahontas to the poet. We are reminded of the star in "Harbor Dawn" that set under a "mistletoe of dreams" and promised to lead the poet-seeker to his goal "at some distant hill." But the star of "Southern Cross" reveals only a "wraith" whom the poet tentatively identifies as "Eve" or "Magdalene" or "Mary," but who eventually emerges as a twentieth-century Eve.

> O simian Venus, homeless Eve,
> Unwedded, stumbling gardenless to grieve
> Windswept guitars on lonely decks forever;
> Finally to answer all within one grave!

This modern Eve is a burlesque of the women mentioned in the first half of *The Bridge*. In "The Dance" Crane spoke of Pocahontas as having "time like a serpent down her shoulder, dark." In "Southern Cross" the contemporary Pocahontas also has a serpent in her hair, but it is a venomous one. Pocahontas has been transformed into Medusa:

> You crept out simmering, accomplished.
> Water rattled that stinging coil, your
> Rehearsed hair—docile, alas, from many arms.
> Yes, Eve—wraith of my unloved seed.

105

The poem then concludes as the constellation disappears with the coming of dawn. Light comes like a sea to submerge the "lithic trillions" of the "spawn" of Eve, of whom the poet is one.

In Melville's poem entitled "Southern Cross" there is a spirit of desolation that is not far removed from the spirit of Crane's similarly entitled poem. Melville's lines testify to the same sense of loss as the poet watches the stars fade in the light of day:

> Translated Cross, hast thou withdrawn,
> Dim paling too at every dawn,
> With symbols vain once counted wise,
> And gods declined to heraldries?

For Crane, as for Melville, the "Cross" and the spectral world which it brought into existence and sustained "buckled" with the dawn. But the spectral world does not disappear before the poet is shown a changed Pocahontas. The "bride" of "The Dance" has become an anonymous prostitute who "lifts her girdles from her, one by one" until the poet's "mind is churned to spittle, whispering hell."

In "National Winter Garden" the "glacier woman" of "The Dance" has been metamorphosed into a strip-teaser in Minsky's famous burlesque show in New York. The strip-teaser shares with Pocahontas the ability to attract, but she differs from Pocahontas in that she frustrates rather than satisfies those whom she does attract. She is dedicated to provocation. Her "buttocks in pink beads" arouse delicious lusts—"Waken salads in the brain"—in the "bandy eyes" of her admirers until she has tranced them into thinking that the world is "one flagrant, sweating cinch."

But this twentieth-century "glacier woman" has nothing of the pristine purity of Pocahontas. Nor does she bear the "pure serpent" of "The Dance." Instead, her attractive serpentine rings, like the lascivious dances she performs on a stage, are a sham.

> And shall we call her whiter than the snow?
> Sprayed first with ruby, then with emerald sheen—
> Least tearful and least glad (who knows her smile?)
> A caught slide shows her sandstone grey between.
>
> Her eyes exist in swivellings of her teats,
> Pearls whip her hips, a drench of whirling strands.
> Her silly snake rings begin to mount, surmount
> Each other—turquoise fakes on tinselled hands.

The strip-teaser's version of Maquokeeta's dance leads not to regeneration but degeneration. She excites unrequitable lusts rather than true passions until she reaches "the lewd trounce of a final muted beat!" As she denudes herself, the members of her audience "flee her spasm through a fleshless door." This is not an image of union but of separation. Her flesh is nothing but an "empty trapeze." This emptiness stems from the fact that her configurations lead to no fruitful consummation; the "trapeze" suggests only a futile swing through the lusts she has aroused. She tantalizes not only the lust of man *for* but the faith of man *in* womanhood so that she can ultimately make a "burlesque" of both. In this way she returns her admirers and followers lifelessly back to life after she has cheated them of the life which they hoped to find in her.

> Yet, to the empty trapeze of your flesh,
> O Magdalene, each comes back to die alone.
> Then you, the burlesque of our lust—and faith,
> Lug us back lifeward—bone by infant bone.

In "Virginia" Pocahontas is a young secretary who coyly repulses the advances of her employer by "smiling the boss away." This secretary, like the prostitute in "Southern Cross" and the strip-teaser in "National Winter Garden," has none of the virginal innocence of Pocahontas, but there is nevertheless something about her that is not Eve-like nor Magdalene-like. On the one hand, she is the poet's Saturday date—"blue-eyed Mary with the claret scarf." On the other hand, she is associated with "Spring in Prince Street." This is not the Cumberland Spring where Pocahontas' "breasts are fanned/O stream by slope and vineyard—into bloom!" On "Prince Street" and "Bleeker" the "daffodils," "slender violets," "peonies," and "forget-me-nots" bloom only on "cornices" and "at windowpanes." These associations suggest that, despite her coyness, there is still a vestige of innocence in this Mary.

Distracted by the sound of "popcorn bells," the poet is suddenly moved to invoke the Mary of the "Ave Maria." He imagines that the Mary who coyly smiles "the boss away" in the "nickle-dime tower" of a modern skyscraper is transformed into the Virgin Mary. Perhaps it is the poet's awareness of her remaining innocence that prompts this association in his mind. Thus "Saturday Mary" becomes "Cathedral Mary," who has already been identified in the first half of *The Bridge* as the mediatrix or bridge between man and God and who will crush the serpent's head in final victory. "Recognizing defeat through Eve, who brought death into the world," writes Bernice Slote, "life is reborn by the accep-

tance of the flesh and generation, begun at its lowest form in Magdalene and rising to the idealized reality of Mary." The positive
value that Slote attaches to the "National Winter Garden" episode
in "Three Songs" may be slightly exaggerated, but the ascent from
Eve through Magdalene to Mary is unmistakable in the three
poems. Moreover, each of these transformations of the Pocahon-
tas-Mary symbol can be related to the image of the bridge as a
woman and thus to the dominant symbol of the entire poem.

VI

QUAKER HILL

In "Quaker Hill" Crane is primarily concerned with dramatizing
the discrepancy between the way the world is and the way that he
thinks it should be. By using epigraphic quotations from Emily
Dickinson and Isadora Duncan, whom he came to admire greatly
after he saw her perform in Cleveland in 1922, Crane prefatorily
suggests how far the real world diverges from the ideal. The quotation from Isadora Duncan is the more explicit of the two epi-
graphs in suggesting this theme in "Quaker Hill": *"I see only the
ideal. But no ideals have ever been fully successful on this earth."*
The idealism and forbearance that characterize this quotation
carry over into the tone of Crane's poem.

Crane first contrasts those people who are "as cows that see no
other thing/Than grass and snow" with those who, like Crane himself and the two women from whose work he has drawn his epi-
graphs, "taste the bright annoy/Of friendship's acid wine." The
former are the tourists who have come to Quaker Hill's "old Mizzentop." They typify the uncultured culture-seekers of the twenties. Crane is less acerbic than H. L. Mencken actually was
toward these Americans, but the values of these people are plain
enough without the need of satire or hyperbole. They either
squint from the "central cupola" of Mizzentop to see "borders of
three states" or distract themselves with bourgeois amusement.
The poet remains unimpressed and uninvolved, being concerned
with the deeper realities of existence.

> But I have seen death's stare in slow survey
> From four horizons that no one relates . . .
> Weekenders avid of their turf-won scores,
> Here three hours from the semaphores, the Czars
> Of golf, by twos and threes in plaid plusfours
> Alight with sticks abristle and cigars.

Crane follows this with sarcastic allusions to some of the vices created by Prohibition ("bootleg roadhouses") and to the shallow contemporary concept of notoriety ("Hollywood's new love-nest pageant"). He then notes how the local citizenry of Quaker Hill have changed the unglamorous "old Meeting House" to the "New Avalon Hotel" in an attempt to attract the touring "highsteppers." Dembo's remark about this image suggests an even greater depth to Crane's satire. Dembo claims that the "full irony of this name can be appreciated when one recalls that Avalon was the ocean isle of Arthurian romance associated with earthly paradise; in quest of Atlantis, the poet finds only the paradise of a tourist hotel."

In the next section Crane loses his satirical edge and becomes so explicit in his castigation of society's fall from the ideal that the poem almost loses its momentum. Indignation usurps the place of inspiration, and poetry becomes little more than heightened rhetoric. Only when he returns to the symbols of the "sundered parentage" of man (Maquokeeta) and the soil (Pocahontas) does Crane regain his artistic balance, although the poem by then has been seriously flawed. Having recaptured his equilibrium, Crane does well to bring the poem to a close. Despite the overt bitterness of the rhetorical sections, the poet does not slide into despair. Instead he finds enough courage to face the autumn of the real world with both faith and patience even while his "heart is rung" by the same Philistinism that "Emily, that Isadora knew."

> While high from dim elm-chancels hung with dew,
> That triple-noted clause of moonlight—
> Yes, whip-poor-will, unhusks the heart of fright,
> Breaks us and saves, yes, breaks the heart, yet yields
> That patience that is armour and that shields
> Love from despair—when love foresees the end—
> Leaf after autumnal leaf
> > break off,
> > > descend—
> > > > descend—

VII
THE TUNNEL

In "The Tunnel" Crane demonstrates the sustained poetic excellence that he achieved in "Proem: To Brooklyn Bridge," "Ave Maria," and "The Dance." Using as his epigraph two lines from William Blake's "Morning" to suggest that man must first pass through a spiritual purgation ("the Gates of Wrath") before he can reach the paradise of Atlantis-Cathay ("the Western Path"), Crane proceeds to find a counterpart for this purgation in a symbolic subway ride through a tunnel under one of New York's rivers. The Dantean implications of this purgatorial subway ride are obvious, but the moral aspect of the poet's purgation in the tunnel and its relation to the theme of the poem that follows "The Tunnel" in *The Bridge* are what sound the "Everlasting No" before the "Everlasting yea" of "Atlantis."

As the poem begins, we meet the poet amid the "congresses" from "Times Square to Columbus Circle." The allusion to Columbus is somewhat ironic here. The discoverer of the North American continent is now only the name of a concourse among the ruck of the "thousand theatres, faces—/Mysterious kitchens." The poet wanders the streets as if drawn to explore these multiple "assortments" ("search them all") before returning to Brooklyn and bed to read "tabloid crime-sheets perched in easy sight."

Undecided about walking home "across the Bridge," as he did in "Cutty Sark," or riding the subway to his flat in Brooklyn, the poet finally permits his sleepiness to "scuttle" his impulse to walk. He decides to be "minimum" and become one of the anonymous millions who ride the subways and whose only moments of self-knowledge come at times when they are isolated in the quadrant of revolving glass doors leading to the trains.

> Be minimum, then, to swim the hiving swarms
> Out of the Square, the Circle burning bright—
> Avoid the glass doors gyring at your right,
> Where boxed alone a second, eyes take fright
> —Quite unprepared rush naked back to light:
> And down beside the turnstile press the coin
> Into the slot. The gongs already rattle.

In the "underground" of the subway's "monotone of motion," the poet pieces together fragments of the world that surrounds him. Crane makes no attempt to unify these fragments; the only order they possess is the questionable order of disarray, but it is this disarray which both indicts and reveals the world of the subway to the observing poet. As in the opening lines of "The River" Crane lets these fragmentary lines in "The Tunnel" speak for themselves to create a picture of the passing scene. This heaping together of apparently disassociated images is simply another testament of Crane's architectonic or "virtuosic" ability to give some meaning even to the seemingly meaningless. "It's almost ghastly, almost surgery," he wrote to Waldo Frank vis-à-vis the manner in which he composed some of these lines, "and, oddly almost all from the notes and stitches I have written while swinging on the strap at late midnights going home." Some of the "notes and stitches" that Crane has woven into the fabric of the poem are snatches of conversation, which are not only disconnected but almost frantic in the overall effect of their simultaneity. These wisps of talk suggest to the poet things that have been frayed by use ("beaten weather vanes") or objects which, though covered by "verdigris," still manage, like hair growing from the scalp of a corpse, to outlast the putrifying flesh that remains as food for its growth. In this underground world of petty greed and overheard crudities, the poet imagines that he hears the "phonographs of hades in the brain." He envisions these subway conversations as "tunnels that re-wind themselves" into a labyrinth of confusion. Even love in the underworld fizzles in a welter of human waste like a "burnt match skating in a urinal":

> "what do you want? getting weak on the links?
> fandaddle daddy don't ask for change—IS THIS
> FOURTEENTH? it's half past six she said—if
> you don't like my gate why did you
> swing on it, why *didja*
> swing on it
> anyhow—"

Amid the combined noises of the subway and the disjointed talk of the passengers Crane suddenly imagines that he sees the face of Edgar Allan Poe. As Whitman is the "saunterer on free ways still ahead," Poe is the one who traverses the lost world below. Horton has explained in convincing detail the many parallels between Poe and Crane, noting how their respective quests for recognition were frustrated, how each verged continually toward destitution, how both suffered from feelings of persecution, how both were given to "insane outbursts of defiant egotism that amounted at times to delusions of grandeur." It is not only appropriate but perhaps inevitable that Crane would meet Poe, his spiritual kinsman in the history of American poetry, in the subterranean world of the subway.

> And why do I often meet your visage here,
> Your eyes like agate lanterns—on and on
> Below the toothpaste and the dandruff ads?
> —And did their riding eyes right through your side,
> And did their eyes like unwashed platters ride?

And Death, aloft,—gigantically down
Probing through you—toward me, O evermore!
And when they dragged your retching flesh,
Your trembling hands that night through Baltimore—
That last night on the ballot rounds, did you
Shaking, did you deny the ticket, Poe?

This passage, though brief, is suffused with Crane's sympathy
for Poe. In the images of "their riding eyes right through your
side" and "unwashed platters" Crane seems to be trying to evoke
memories of Christ and John the Baptist in order to link the fate
of Poe and his own fate with the fate of a defeated savior or a
sacrificed prophet.

As the subway train prepares to cross "the final level for the
dive" beneath the river, the poet sees Columbus prefigured in a
Genoese "washerwoman" and asks rhetorically if she brings love
and beauty back to her children after a day of cleaning the "corridors" and "cuspidors" of the "gaunt sky-barracks." This sardonic question becomes a preface to the poem's final notes of despair and the desperate, agonizing hope of the conclusion. Crane
sees the tunnel as a "Dæmon" that swallows everything in a "de-
murring and eventful yawn." It muffles the "conscience" of the
poet ("umbilical to call") before he can struggle against "the
plunging wind." In this image the tunnel assumes the symbolic
character that Crane ascribed to it in a letter to Otto Kahn when
he described it as an "encroachment of machinery on humanity."
Men and women are whirled "like pennies beneath soot and
stream" and precipitated blindly through the "shrill ganglia" of
the underground networks of the subway. But while the poet
himself is caught helplessly in the Dæmon's grasp ("Kiss of our
agony thou gatherest"), he still feels, "like Lazarus," the possibility of resurrection as the train climbs the river bottom toward the
opposite shore. He looks for a release from the underworld by the
intercession of the "Word" of the poetic imagination. In "Voyages VI" Crane used the same image and referred to the "Word"
as the "unbetrayable reply/Whose accent no farewell can know."
In the concluding lines of "The Tunnel" he again invokes the sav-
ing power of the same "Word":

And yet, like Lazarus, to feel the slope,
The sod and billow breaking,—lifting ground,
—A sound of waters bending astride the sky
Unceasing with some Word that will not die . . . !

As Columbus stood on the deck of his ship and looked out over the ocean in the "Ave Maria," the poet stands on the shores of Brooklyn after he has debouched from the subway and watches a "tugboat" cross the river and leave in its settling wake an "oily tympanum of waters." Having passed through "the Gates of Wrath" and emerged into the open air, the poet feels capable of discovering the "Western path" to Atlantis. He resigns himself to the future—"Tomorrow"—and lets his "hands drop memory" into the waters of the river of time. Thus freed of anticipation and retrospect, Crane is able to rebuff the Dæmonic "kiss of our agony" with the awesome prayer and epithet that Columbus used to conclude the "Ave Maria":

> Kiss of our agony Thou gatherest,
> O Hand of Fire
> gatherest—

VIII

ATLANTIS

If the "Atlantis" reminds us of the excellence of the best poems in the first half of *The Bridge,* it is because Crane wrote the poem during the fruitful period of his stay on the Isle of Pines in 1925. "Atlantis" sprang from the same moment that spawned "Proem: To Brooklyn Bridge," "Ave Maria," and "Powhatan's Daughter." When Crane sent the poem to Waldo Frank on August 3, 1926, he could not keep from saying that he felt he was "dancing on dynamite these days" and that he "didn't realize that a bridge is begun from the two ends at once." It was when Crane sought to fuse the ends that he occasionally faltered, as in parts of "Cape Hatteras" and "Quaker Hill," which are members of a different poetic generation. However, in its position as the concluding poem of *The Bridge,* the "Atlantis" does much to save the second half of the sequence from falling too far below the achievement of the first half.

In the first stanza of "Atlantis" the bridge appears as a huge harp that resounds with the music that Plato called *"the knowledge of that which/relates to love in harmony and system."* We have been prepared for this figure by Crane's use of the word "harp" as a synonym for the bridge in the "Proem: To Brooklyn Bridge." In "Atlantis" the music of knowledge that proceeds from the harp is transformed into a "steeled Cognizance." In the "flight of strings" of the bridge-harp, a number of "sybilline voices flicker" to give a further hint of the capacity of the bridge to "lend a myth to God"—"as though a god were issue of the strings."

The poet sees the bridge as a single "arc" over the river of time below it ("labyrinthine mouths of history") as well as over the numberless voyages of "all ships at sea." The "curveship" thus becomes a variation of the rainbow-symbol in "Voyages," and the lost continent of Atlantis becomes the goal of the poet as a modern discoverer in the sense in which Belle Isle was the goal of the poet as voyager. Both Atlantis and Belle Isle are Crane's symbols for poetic truth and beauty. He reached Belle Isle by voyaging on the sea of time and hopes to reach Atlantis via the bridge of the poetic imagination. He is animated by the same spirit that compelled Columbus in "Ave Maria" to discover the secret of Cathay. The spirit is identical; only the goal has changed.

The image of the bridge-harp is continued in the allusion to "arching strands of song" and "humming spars" suspended between the bridge's "twin monoliths." Letting his eyes follow the bridge's "loft of vision, palladium helm of stars," the poet feels himself "propelled by glistening fins of light" to cross with his own consciousness the gap between time and eternity. In "The Dance" the Indian-poet (Maquokeeta) resolved the dichotomy between the "eagle" and the "serpent" by uniting himself with the earth (Pocahontas). In "Atlantis" the resolution of a deeper problem is involved. The poet must assume the role of prophet. He must discover how far the "real" has diverged from the "ideal" in order to fulfill, as he urged the aviator to do in "Cape Hatteras," the "Sanskrit charge/to conjugate infinity's dim marge—/Anew!" The problem exceeds the spatiotemporal one of trying to fuse the best of two cultures. It demands the linking of the "cipher-script of time" with the "timeless laugh of mythic spears"—the vitalization of the finite world by the poetic vision.

> Sheerly the eyes, like seagulls stung with rime—
> Slit and propelled by glistening fins of light—
> Pick biting way up towering looms that press
> Sidelong with flight of blade on tendon blade
> —Tomorrows into yesteryear—and link
> What cipher-script of time no traveller reads
> But who, through smoking pyres of love and death,
> Searches the timeless laugh of mythic spears.

Though the subsequent stanza is rife with obscurity, it can be best understood as an ascent through time to the "white, pervasive Paradigm" of love. The poet is here striving to dramatize his quest to reach the Cathay-Belle Isle-Atlantis of the "imaged Word." He seems to be wrestling language to his purposes as a mystic would have to rely on the metaphorical character of language to describe an almost indescribable moment of ecstasy in which he felt himself drawn toward a more intimate union with God.

Crane compares his struggle to gain the Absolute of Atlantis to the quest of Jason for the golden fleece. Having read "The Tunnel," we are aware of the poet's struggle with the "Dæmon" of the subway that preceded his discovery of "the Western path." Similarly, Jason and the Argonauts had to evade a watchful dragon that guarded the fleece before they could attain their goal. Thus Jason, like the poet in "Atlantis," had to pursue the object of his search "right thro' the Gates of Wrath."

> And you, aloft there—Jason! hesting Shout!
> Still wrapping harness to the swarming air!
> Silvery the rushing wake, surpassing call,
> Beams yelling Æolus! splintered in the straits!

Like Jason, Crane will continue his quest. In the world of the new "Tyre" and the new "Troy," Crane still sees the bridge of the poetic imagination, as he did in the "Proem," as the only force capable of "lifting night to cycloramic crest/Of deepest day." In the "Proem" Crane spoke of the bridge as the "threshold of the prophet's pledge,/Prayer of pariah, and the lover's cry." In "Atlantis" he has crossed the threshold, and the pledge, prayer and cry receive their answer in the "choiring strings" that "mere toil" could never "align."

> O Choir, translating time
> Into what multitudinous Verb the suns
> And synergy of waters ever fuse, recast
> In myriad syllables,—Psalm of Cathay!
> O Love, thy white, pervasive Paradigm . . . !

This stanza and the one that follows it are not, as Waggoner has suggested, poetic statements "which appear to sing the praises of tall buildings." Nor are they simply an adulterated Whitmanlike vision of the "United States of the future," as Winters has charged. What they really afford is a reaffirmation of the synthesizing power of the poetic imagination to give direction to the work of a "trillion whispering hammers" and the "long anvil cry." Crane means that only the bridge of the poetic imagination ("O harp and altar, of the fury fused") is capable of transcending this

century's "pangs of dust and steel," of integrating man's ingenuity
with material into the "unfractioned idiom" of the "imaged Word,"
of being the "vernal strophe" that "chimes from deathless strings."

> O Thou steeled Cognizance whose leap commits
> The agile precincts of the lark's return;
> Within whose lariat sweep encinctured sing
> In single chrysalis the many twain,—
> Of stars Thou art the stitch and stallion glow
> And like an organ, Thou, with sound of doom—
> Sight, sound and flesh Thou leadest from time's realm
> As love strikes clear direction for the helm.

The poet then claims that the "intrinsic Myth" of the bridge
and its redemptive promise exist not only in the "bright drench
and fabric of our veins" but in all of nature—"ripe fields/Revolv-
ing through their harvests in sweet torment." The implication
of the image is decidedly pantheistic, but we cannot forget that
Crane, like Shelley, had a cosmic conception of poetry's function
and poetry's power. This power, according to Crane, could save
man from the dæmonic tragedy of the tunnel; it could animate all
nature with its vitality. Possibly for this reason Crane identifies
it as a gift from God, transfigurative in its potentialities and
apocalyptic and eternal in its very nature.

> Forever Deity's glittering Pledge, O Thou
> Whose canticle fresh chemistry assigns
> To rapt inception and beatitude,—
> Always through blinding cables, to our joy,
> Of thy white seizure springs the prophecy:
> Always through spiring cordage, pyramids
> Of silver sequel, Deity's young name
> Kinetic of white choiring wings . . . ascends.

The penultimate stanza of "Atlantis" is strongly reminiscent of
"Voyages II." Like the voyager who sails the "rimless floods" of
time and asks to be spared the "earthly shore" of death until he
learns the answer to the "seal's wide spindrift gaze toward paradise," the poet-seeker of "Atlantis" is involved in journeys that
"must needs void memory." He asks to be held in the "vortex"
of the "Anemone" or "Atlantis" because it is the "Answerer of all."
Atlantis here is not only a counterpart of Belle Isle—the world of
truth and beauty as perceived by the imagination; it is also a
further elaboration of all that is suggested by Cathay—the world
that is the object of quest and awaits discovery. By being related

to Belle Isle and Cathay, Atlantis is inevitably related to the
bridge itself considered as a "symbol of consciousness, knowledge,
spiritual unity."

> So to thine Everpresence, beyond time,
> Like spears ensanguined of one tolling star
> That bleeds infinity—the orphic strings,
> Sidereal phalanxes, leap and converge:
> One Song, one Bridge of Fire! . . .

In these concluding lines Crane is still addressing the bridge
directly. As a symbol of the poetic imagination or of "consciousness spanning time and space," the bridge is "beyond time"
although its "orphic strings" are bathed in the blood of time—
"one tolling star." The allusion to Orpheus is particularly noteworthy since the poet in "The Tunnel" has survived the Orphean
experience of returning from the underworld to the "lifting
ground." But even though the "Everpresence" of the bridge will
persist as "One Song, one Bridge of Fire," the poet is compelled to
end the "Atlantis" and *The Bridge* not with an alleluia but with a
question:

> Is it Cathay,
> Now pity steeps the grass and rainbows ring
> The serpent with the eagle in the leaves . . . ?
> Whispers antiphonal in azure swing.

The poet asks this concluding question as much of himself as
of the bridge. Has he found the answer that will reconcile the
"serpent" and the "eagle" in a world where the tunnel and the
bridge exist simultaneously? It is interesting to note here that
"The Dance" concludes with the same images of "serpent" and
"eagle" but in an affirmative rather than an interrogative statement. The image of "serpent" and "eagle" in "Atlantis" is part
of a question, and there remains some doubt about the possibility
of finding an answer—at least, no answer is given. The only response comes in the "swing" of whispers in the sky. Bernice Slote
suggests that this line conveys "the balanced poise of the present,
whose moment of Here and Now is what we know of the bridge of
consciousness." If Slote's interpretation is correct, it would seem
that the sky-whispers are really not answers at all, unless one
thinks that the equilibrium of consciousness is an answer.

If the poet's question is unanswered and possibly unanswer-
able, the spiritual quest of the second half of *The Bridge* has
ended on the same note as the spatiotemporal quest of the first

half. If the final lines of "Cutty Sark," which concludes the first half, and those of "Atlantis," which concludes the second half, are questions, it could possibly be that Crane means that the question is more important than the answer. Indeed, there may be no answer to the question of reconciling time and eternity, as there may be no way to stifle the imaginative quest that the poet is eternally impelled to make. The important thing is that the question is asked and the quest undertaken. In effect, *The Bridge* is a dramatization of the question and the quest. It is not a poem of discovery as much as it is a poem of pilgrimage. Cathay and Atlantis will always invite those with the courage to venture. Man will eternally strive for the "imaged Word" of truth and beauty in the world of his own consciousness. In this sense, Cathay and Atlantis are not destinations; they are motivations. This may be the deepest theme of *The Bridge*. If the poem is a dramatization of a search, it could well be that Crane is insisting that the true meaning of the search is not in the thing sought, but in the seeking.

In reading *The Bridge,* as in reading most of the poems of Crane's third and most mature period, it is necessary to "read" with more senses than the eye. This becomes an almost indispensable prerequisite when one realizes that Crane was a poet whose concern for language was multidimensional. Words created for him a beauty that transcended both their denotative and connotative meaning; this beauty arose from the sounds of words both singly and together, from the feelings created by sound as well as sense and, finally, from the often unnoticed texture of the alphabetical pigment itself. Crane exploited each of these capacities of language. Horton has recorded how Crane "gloried in words aside from their meanings in themselves, prizing their weight, density, color, and sound; and gloated over the subtle multiplicity of their associations—'the so-called illogical impingements of the connotations of words on the consciousness.' " Nor was Crane unaware of the melodic capabilities of language. Horton has noted with particular emphasis that Crane "was obsessed by a desire to approach poetry to the condition of music." These aspects of Crane's talent can be found in some of the best poems in *White Buildings*, and they carry over into the best poems in *The Bridge.*

Crane's proclivities to raise poetry to the levels of painting and music are important to any one who is concerned with achieving a full grasp of Crane's work. The reader must be ready to admit that what is obscure to the eye may not be obscure to the ear. Where the reason balks, there must the imagination venture. But this venture must not only be a visual one. The imagination must be similarly keyed to the effects produced on the other senses. Nor is such an approach unreasonable. Just as the poetic process itself is not always reducible to ratiocinative terms, so is the fruit of that process similarly irreducible. One must learn to proceed with all senses alerted and let the language of the poet impress the senses with those hidden capabilities of language which the poet himself has had to discover or invent in order to put his vision into words.

To say that the reader must approach *The Bridge* with all his senses alerted is not to say that the poem is simply a congeries of sensations. There is such a thing as "intelligenciated sense," to borrow the language of Jacques Maritain, and it is this suffusion of the senses by the power of intellect that is at the heart of Crane's talent in *The Bridge*. A critic who ignores these idiosyncratic aspects of poetic talent does so at the risk of imperiling his understanding of much of Crane's poetry. James E. Miller, Jr., is one critic who has shown a proper awareness of this fact. This is affirmed in Miller's conviction that

> Crane asserted that as a poet he is more concerned with the "illogical impingements of the connotations of words on the consciousness" than with "the preservation of their logically rigid significations." This concept gives rise to the terms "dynamics of metaphor" or "logic of metaphor," by which Crane means the metaphorical language charged by a complex of "emotional connectives" that are not grasped by the intellect but felt in the depths of the mind where "thought" becomes "feeling."

Miller is simply reconstructing Crane's aesthetic so that any criticisms of the poet's work will be undertaken with a full awareness of the way his poems came to be and how they should be read.

The failure of many to understand Crane's aesthetic has resulted in a number of misinterpretations of *The Bridge*. The most untenable of these approaches is the one that bases its condemnation of the poem on the fact that Crane himself felt a growing sense of failure about it. The fallacy of this approach is rooted in the spurious tendency to justify one's estimate of a poem by the author's feelings toward it. This is particularly vulnerable in the case of Crane since he suffered from a lifelong sense of failure. Following such an approach to its logical conclusion would mean discarding almost all of Crane's poems as worthless. But such an approach cannot be called critical any more than it can be called literary. One would not scrap the *Summa Theologica* simply because St. Thomas Aquinas is reported to have said on one occasion that the entire effort of writing it was worthless. Nor would one destroy the ceiling of the Sistine Chapel because Michelangelo in his dotage felt that his creations were fit only for sledge-hammering.

The second misrepresentation is revealed in some of the critical comments of Allen Tate, Brom Weber, and Yvor Winters on *The Bridge*. Each of these critics regards the poem as a failure. Tate, while conceding the beauty of certain passages of lyrical excellence, is convinced that the work fails because Crane was unable to handle a theme that transcended "single moments in the stream of consciousness." [3] Weber finds fault with *The Bridge* for a similar reason when he says that "Crane did both himself and poetry less good when he underestimated the expression of personal emotion as a legitimate phase of art and attempted to create single-handed a philosophical and sociological myth in which, as it happened, personal emotion predominated when it should not have." Yvor Winters insists that the poem is a failure because it is "loosely constructed" and that "incomprehensibility and looseness of construction are the natural result of the theme, which is inherited from Whitman and Emerson." The result of this, according to Winters, is that the "style is at worst careless and pretentious, at second-best skillfully obscure; and in these respects it is religiously of its school; and although it is both sound and powerful at its best, it is seldom at its best."

The criticisms of Tate, Weber, and Winters either tend to measure the poem against the most literal standards of history, by the critic's own estimate of how Crane failed to realize his donneé or by predetermined aesthetic criteria applied inorganically to the poem. One cannot help but feel that these critics take Crane to task for what he did not or what they feel he could not do instead of dealing with the less subjunctive matter of what he actually did. This, of course, does not invalidate all of their comments, which offer much that is both valuable and correct, but it does indicate that they may have prevented themselves from seeing the poem in its own rather than in their own terms. Geoffrey Moore has suggested what may be the real cause of Tate's disagreement with Crane in *The Bridge,* and, in so doing, he has suggested where

[3] *The Man of Letters in the Modern World* (New York: Meridian, 1955).

critics similar in approach to Tate run the risk of error in dealing with a poet like Crane:

> Alan Tate, while conceding the excellence of individual passages,
> considers the poem as a whole "a failure in the sense that *Hyperion*
> is a failure, and with comparable magnificence." Mr. Tate's con-
> clusion has been generally adopted, but it is essentially classical
> criticism of a romantic poet. Judged in terms of what he was try-
> ing to do rather than what his critics think he ought to have done
> Crane's poem may be seen as a huge attempt to display the many
> facets of the modern consciousness. For such a purpose the tight,
> ordered structure and relatively simple theme of the traditional
> epic is inappropriate.[4]

Opposed to the positions of Tate, Weber, and Winters are critics
like Hyatt Waggoner, Sister Bernetta Quinn, Bernice Slote, and,
most recently, L. S. Dembo. These critics avoid considering *The
Bridge* in a purely historical or philosophical sense, and they also
do not measure Crane's final achievement against his early, self-
defined Pindaric obligation to give a poetic reconciliation of all the
discordant factors in the "machine age, so called." The position
of these critics is basically that one does not criticize the farmer's
soil before commenting on the quality of the farmer's wheat. The
quality of the wheat is what is primarily important. In this regard, writes Waggoner,

> One need not share Whitman's and Crane's mystical pantheism in
> order to acknowledge that their aim was lofty. One need not be-
> lieve that a religious myth for our time must be created, not re-
> discovered; or that the first step in its creation must be the "af-
> firmation" of the sum total of the American past and present, the
> second a "transcending" of these facts; or that man's increasing
> technological mastery over nature is a good symbol of his increas-
> ing spiritual health and closeness to God—one need not agree with
> these ideas or share these attitudes in order to believe that the sub-
> ject of *The Bridge* was the most important that can well be im-
> agined, and that the insight that prompted Crane to undertake the
> poem was an act of genius.

Waggoner's statement is indeed an important critical assumption
to make for the simple reason that it is prompted by the "poetic
faith" that makes criticism possible. It does not guarantee unqualified praise of the poem in question. As a matter of fact,
Waggoner finds many unresolved contradictions in *The Bridge*

[4] *The Penguin Book of Modern American Verse* (Baltimore: Penguin,
1954).

and considers the poem weakened because of them. Nevertheless, his reservations are derived from a study of the poem itself and not from a priori positions nor from an aesthetic or ethical bias. Similar "willing suspensions of disbelief" have been made by Sister Bernetta Quinn and Bernice Slote. Sister Bernetta Quinn's critique of *The Bridge* stems from her willingness to share Crane's "logic of imagination—akin to that of dreams and hence to metamorphosis." Bernice Slote analyzes Crane's admiration of Whitman and makes this the basis for her acceptance of Crane's aesthetic:

> Since Crane so clearly took the Whitman position, he will be misunderstood as long as that position is misunderstood. If Whitman is seen as a bubbling exploiter of American chauvinism, *The Bridge* will seem like a hapless panegyric of American history and science, with many of the individual poems obviously unconnected. If, however, Whitman is seen as a deeply spiritual thinker, a mystic of cosmic consciousness . . . the pattern in *The Bridge* has a chance to come into focus. And it is critical here to note that whatever any one else may think of Whitman, Crane considered him a mystic of a particular oneness. The shape of *The Bridge* derives from that principle.

Not far removed from Slote's position is that of L. S. Dembo. Dembo claims that the unifying principle of the poem derives in part from Whitman's influence upon Crane but primarily from the influence of Nietzsche. The proposition of *The Bridge* is that

> society holds within it the possibility of its own redemption, not that it has already been redeemed. The technology that has produced the subway and what it stands for can also produce the Bridge, but modern man will stay on the subway until the poet leads him to the Bridge, speaks the Word that holds his vision of the Absolute. Society will be redeemed when it understands its tragic nature and through its imagination, which speaks through the poet, moves beyond tragedy to a knowledge of divinity.

Even though critics like Tate, Weber, Winters, Waggoner, Quinn, Slote, and Dembo approach *The Bridge* from opposite shores, they are all agreed that the poem is one of quest. The basic point of disagreement arises from their conceptions of what the poet was seeking. This has led to misinterpretations about the nature of the poem, which in turn has tended to distort its real value.

If, as some of Crane's critics have suggested, *The Bridge* is weakened by passages where the meters seem forced and the images willed into position, it was not because of the faltering of Crane's lyric talent in the face of an epic challenge. If an epic is regarded in part as the testament of a people or a culture, *The Bridge* is simply not an epic, despite the persistence of some critics to treat it and subsequently condemn it as such and despite Crane's early Pindaric ambitions for it. Instead, *The Bridge* is the personal testament of one twentieth-century poet within the framework of his own and his country's past, present, and future as they appeared to him. The symbols that Hart Crane chose from various periods of American history and literature to incarnate his vision have their true meaning in their relationship to him. They are, we must assume, those things that appeared significant to Crane's sensibility. Their hierarchic importance in the historical sense is not in question here. The primitivistic themes of "The Dance" or Crane's Nietzschean faith in the poet as a type of redemptive hero in "Cape Hatteras" and "Atlantis" may or may not be regarded as crucial aspects of American culture, but they were to Crane. As such, they are reflective of his own vision. Thus the success or failure of some parts of *The Bridge* cannot be made answerable to any other criterion but their success or failure as poetry. If we discuss the work in terms of history, we are measuring the poem by a nonpoetic standard. If we discuss the poem in terms of its inadequacy as an American epic, we are ignoring its true nature and attempting to judge it as something which it most certainly is not. In the same sense, if passages in *The Bridge* fail at times because the lines seem "manufactured" and the poetic moments adulterated by rhetoric, it is simply because manufactured lines and adulterated poetic moments are never consistent with good poetry. Crane was as vulnerable to such lapses as any poet, and we must criticize him in that context. Occasional lapses should not blind us to the true significance of *The Bridge* as a revelation of Crane's sensibility coming to terms with itself and the world confronting it.

6

∾§ THE BROKEN WORLD

Eᴠxᴄᴇᴘᴛ for a handful of poems in *Key West: An Island Sheaf*
this final collection of Crane's work does not contribute sig-
nificantly to his poetic stature. Poems like "Island Quarry," "The
Mermen," "The Idiot," "A Name for All," "Bacardi Spreads the
Eagle's Wings," "And Bees of Paradise," "To Emily Dickinson,"
"Moment Fugue," "To the Cloud Juggler," "By Nilus Once I
Knew," and "Old Song" are scarcely distinguishable in technique
and tone from such poems in *White Buildings* as "Legend," "Black
Tambourine," "My Grandmother's Love Letters," and "Repose of
Rivers." Some of these poems challenge but do not surpass the
excellence of some of the best short lyrics in *White Buildings*.
"To the Cloud Juggler" and "To Emily Dickinson" do not ap-
proach, for example, the beauty and poignance of "Praise for an
Urn" and "At Melville's Tomb," though all four poems are elegiac
memoirs. Of the remaining poems in *Key West: An Island Sheaf*,
"The Mango Tree" is interesting only because of its Dadaist inno-
vations. The pidgin impressionism of "Imperator Victus" is more
of a preface than a complete poem.

"The Hurricane," which was prompted by Crane's observation
of the hurricane that destroyed his retreat on the Isle of Pines, is a
beautiful study of the power of God as suggested by the strength
of tremendous winds. This association of God and the hurricane is
carried on as a dominant symbol in other poems in *Key West*.
Considering the poem technically, R. P. Blackmur claims that
" 'The Hurricane' derives immediately from the metric of Hop-

kins," but Horton denies the metrical influence of Hopkins on "The Hurricane," maintaining that Crane was unaware of Hopkins until 1928, a year after Crane had already written an early version of the poem. However, this does not preclude the fact that alterations may have been made before the final version of the poem was published in 1931. Weber notes, for instance, that Carl Schmitt, the painter who befriended Crane in New York in 1916, "analyzed the work of Dante, Hopkins, and other poets and interested Crane in their ideas and technique." In brief, the metrical influence of Hopkins on "The Hurricane" is revealed in Crane's use of four accentual stresses to the line instead of relying on the usual syllabic measures. As a tone poem with Blake-like overtones, "The Hurricane" is a stirring and successful lyric. "To Shakespeare" has about the same value as "Emblems of Conduct," both being variations by Crane of poems by other poets. The tone poem called "March" shows the continuing influence of the Imagists on Crane. It succeeds in capturing the "waning" of March, but it reveals only a peripheral aspect of Crane's talent.

This survey of some of the poems in *Key West: An Island Sheaf* should not suggest that the book does not deserve serious attention. Even if it is true that there are many poems that contribute little to our understanding of Crane's talent and to our final estimate of him as a poet, there are at least six poems in this book that could stand among the best poems that Crane ever wrote. Of these six, "The Broken Tower" is possibly one of his most consummate achievements.

᪷ᔚ   ᔒᔚ

In "Key West," the title poem of the book, Crane speaks as an exile from the world of the tunnel and the bridge. "Key West" is a poem of retreat. Strengthened by a "salient faith," the poet has come "out of the valley" to "impartial" skies. The world that he now inhabits does not "disown me/Nor claim me." He is, momentarily at least, a refugee from the world of man ("Adam's spine") and woman ("rib").

"Key West" takes up a theme that Crane first introduced in "Legend," the poem that begins *White Buildings*. In "Key West" the poet feels the same call to bring the legend of his "youth into the noon" of life. He discovers a harmony between his flesh ("wrist and bicep") and the cosmos ("the meteorite's white arch"). He feels a strong dedication to "strike a single march" to "heaven or hades—to an equally frugal noon."

125

The final two stanzas focus upon the difference between the poet in retreat and those "millions" who must remain the apparent victims of the city's materialism and avarice. The poet concedes that the victory of the city over man seems to be total. He can think of no one or no place that has not been "sold" or hermetically sealed ("tinned") by the stifling desires for gain or conformity.

> Because these millions reap a dead conclusion
> Need I presume the same fruit of my bone
> As draws them towards a doubly mocked confusion
> Of apish nightmares into steel-strung stone?
>
> O, steel and stone! But gold was, scarcity before.
> And here is water, and a little wind . . .
> There is no breath of friends and no more shore
> Where gold has not been sold and conscience tinned.

The poem "The Phantom Bark" could be a scion of "Cutty Sark." In the first stanza the poet identifies himself as a "drowned man" who chooses to speak again of the times when ships could "trick back the leisured winds." But the age of such voyaging is now past, and the great sailing ships exist only in dreams where each is transformed into a "phantom bark." But the irony of the poem arises from the fact that in this series of a drowned man's dreams there is no possibility of failure; the ghostly ships will always brave the seas of memory and "dream no land in vain."

> Of old there was a promise, and thy sails
> Have kept no faith but wind, the cold stream
> —The hot fickle wind, the breath of males
> Imprisoned never, no not soot or rain.

Poems like "Royal Palm" and "The Air Plant" are notable because they reveal how appropriately the fecundity of the equatorial climate and the tropical plants found a perfect counterpart in the fecundity of Crane's idiom. But these poems are important not only in terms of imagery. They are more than descriptive lyrics. In "Royal Palm," for example, the tree that Crane has chosen to contemplate assumes a symbolic value when he describes it as "the sun's most gracious anchorite." This phrase appears in the poem after Crane's description of the tree as a "tower of whispered light" from which "regal charities/Drift coolly." The combined effect of these two figures suggests that the palm tree is both apart from and somehow superior to all other growing things that surround it in the "noontide's blazed asperities." It is in this spirit that Crane predicates a sense of timelessness of the tree.

> Climb up as by communings, year on year
> Uneaten of the earth or aught earth holds,
> And the grey trunk, that's elephantine, rear
> Its frondings sighing in ætherial folds.

As an anchorite the palm tree is not only forever "fruitless" but removed from and timelessly above "that yield/Of sweat the jungle presses with hot love." It becomes a symbol of immortality "ascending emerald-bright" to eternity itself—"Unshackled, casual of its azured height/As though it soared suchwise through heaven too." The palm tree is thus Crane's tropical bridge, serving the same purpose in Crane's imagination as the bridge in "Atlantis" and suggesting the same transcendence.

"The Air Plant," like "Royal Palm," also moves beyond mere description; the images in the poem come to acquire symbolic meaning. Basically the air plant is only a "tuft that thrives on saline nothingness." It is like an "inverted octopus." It is "pulmonary to the wind," and its lung-like "tentacles" are "horrific in their lurch."

Different from the other cactus plants, which secrete a "milk of earth when stricken off the stalk," the air plant "defenseless, thornless, sheds no blood." But disregarding its apparent insignificance and its lack of defense, Crane calls the plant an "Angelic Dynamo! Ventriloquist of the Blue!" He uses these appositives primarily because the plant receives and is in consonance with winds that have the capacity to be either mere breezes or great hurricanes. The air plant has the capacity to be "pulmonary" to both. Thus it becomes, like the tree of the mustard seed, insignificant at first but capable finally of being what no other tree can be. Ironically, in the very paltriness of the air plant lurks its true power:

> While beachward creeps the shark-swept Spanish Main
> By what conjunctions do the winds appoint
> Its apotheosis, at last—the hurricane!

If there are parallels between the symbolic air plant and the poet, the relationship is best suggested by the hurricane. In many of the poems in *Key West: An Island Sheaf* the hurricane is often used to suggest the power of an awesome divinity. As the air plant is dependent upon the wind for its very life, so Crane suggests that the poet is dependent upon the "apotheosis" of the hurricane of divine inspiration for his.

More subtle and provocative variations of tropical imagery appear in "O Carib Isle." Crane has said that he wrote the poem on "one hellish hot day" while he was living at his grandmother's plantation on the Isle of Pines. Even if he had never written this biographical footnote to the poem, it would be difficult for any sensitive reader not to feel the torpor conveyed by Crane's images and rhythms.

The poem begins with a description of the "tarantula" and "fiddler crabs" as they patrol a beach that the poet regards as a huge grave for "nacreous frames of tropic death":

> The tarantula rattling at the lily's foot
> Across the feet of the dead, laid in white sand
> Near the coral beach—nor zigzag fiddler crabs
> Side-stilting from the path (that shift, subvert
> And anagrammatize your name)—No, nothing here
> Below the palsy that one eucalyptus lifts
> In wrinkled shadows—mourns.

Pausing to remark that the fertile-sounding names of the tropical trees and flowers seem to mock the beach's "brittle crypt," the poet is prompted to speak his own "fertile names" to the "white sand." But he finds himself unable to breathe a word against the heat; he is like the wind that "coils and withdraws" in a sudden silence. In this moment of apparent inability to stay the advance of "tropic death," the poet turns to God. Identifying God both as the "Captain of the doubloon isle/Without a turnstile" and as the "Commissioner of the mildew throughout the ambushed senses," the poet asks if even He is present in this Caribbean jungle. The questions are never answered, of course, but they lead the poet to the poem's sardonic conclusion.

Receiving no answer from the divinity, the poet seeks to be freed from the torpor that surrounds him until his "ghost" shall confront God—"the blue's comedian host." His desire is not so much for death as for ascension. He hopes for a transmigration of spirit that will somehow contradict the omnipresence of death on the beach. He asks to be spared a death similar to the "slow evisceration" of overturned turtles that are left "spiked" at "daybreak on the wharf."

But the poet realizes that this desire for ascension is contradicted by his own earth-bound nature. Consequently, he comes

to regard himself as so much residue left by the hurricane to
atrophy on a volcanic isle whose only possible god is Satan.

> Slagged on the hurricane—I, cast within its flow,
> Congeal by afternoons here, satin and vacant.
> You have given me the shell, Satan,—carbonic amulet
> Sere of the sun exploded in the sea.

⋖⋗ ⋗⋖

Crane's best poem in *Key West: An Island Sheaf* is "The
Broken Tower." It is not only a memorable poetic achievement;
it is Crane's last will and testament, containing that moment of
sudden brightness that came to him before his suicide. In it there
is the poetic power and versatility that reveal Crane at his very
best. It would not be rash to say that "The Broken Tower" is to
Key West: An Island Sheaf what "For the Marriage of Faustus
and Helen" and "Voyages" are to *White Buildings* and what
"Proem: To Brooklyn Bridge," "Ave Maria," "The Dance," "The
Tunnel," and "Atlantis" are to *The Bridge.*

Although Crane sent incomplete versions of "The Broken
Tower" to Peggy Baird, Solomon Grunberg, and Samuel Loveman,
he did not really complete the poem until a month before his
death. The complete version of the poem that he sent to *Poetry*
magazine was mailed on March 25, 1932. Despite Gorham Munson's suspicion that the poem belonged to an early period of
Crane's development, Lesley Simpson, a history professor from
the University of California and Crane's friend during those final
months, has written that the inspiration for the poem undoubtedly
came to Crane in Taxco in late January of 1932.[1] This means
that Crane tooled the poem into its final form in less than two
months, and the final version shows that Crane had regained the
power he had shown in "Voyages" and those poems of *The Bridge*
that he wrote on the Isle of Pines. Simpson's account of the experience that was the poem's genesis is worth quoting in this regard:

I was with Hart Crane in Taxco, Mexico the morning of January
27, this year when he first conceived the idea of "The Broken
Tower." The night before, being troubled with insomnia, he had
risen before daybreak and walked down to the village square. It so
happened that one of the innumerable Indian fiestas was to be
celebrated that day, and Hart met the old Indian bell-ringer who

[1] Peggy Baird also lends support to this position in an article in *Venture,*
IV (1961).

was on his way down to the Church. He and Hart were old friends, and he brought Hart up into the tower with him to help ring the bells. As Hart was swinging the clapper of the great bell, half drunk with its mighty music, the swift tropical dawn broke over the mountains. The sublimity of the scene and the thunder of the bells worked in Hart one of those gusts of joy of which only he was capable. He came striding up the hill afterwards in a sort of frenzy, refused his breakfast, and paced up and down the porch impatiently waiting for me to finish my coffee. Then he seized my arm and bore me off to the plaza where we sat in the shadow of the Church, Hart the while pouring out a magnificent cascade of words.[2]

The zest that Simpson's account ascribes to Crane on that January morning in Taxco was to be tempered in the finished poem by Crane's growing loss of confidence in his own power as a poet. In the final version of the poem, therefore, we have a blend of fire and ice; "The Broken Tower" is simultaneously a dirge and an epiphany. What is revealed is not only the naked spirit of Crane in near despair but also his commitment of poetry as his final hope of salvation. In its agony the poem recalls the beauty of Hopkins' "terrible sonnets" and the last poems of Keats; in its hope of redemption there is an echo of Shelley's "The Cloud." Crane's poem reveals the poet polarized, that is, crucified on the cross of his suffering as well as on the cross of his hope.

The dominant symbol of the poem is the tower, but it is important to remember at the outset that this is a broken tower. If this tower symbolizes the poet, it suggests not only the creative but the destructive aspect of his talent. It perpetuates, too, the Dionysiac, Orphean, and Christ-like symbols that are common to poems like "Lachrymae Christi" and "The Dance"—the concept of the poet as one who sacrifices himself in the very act of creation as his entire being yields to the higher necessity of poetic expression. Like a candlewick that burns brightly only as it burns itself down, the poet's moment of creation is always destructive of something within him that made this fire of creation burn, if only for a moment.

The first two stanzas of the poem are descriptive of the actual tower in Taxco. At the first signs of morning the poet walks on "the cathedral lawn," his "feet chill on steps from hell." The allusion to hell suggests the misery of daily life in the swelter of the tropics as well as the spiritual swelter from which the poet is

[2] *New English Weekly* (September 15, 1932).

momentarily in flight. The use of hell also contrasts with the spiritual world symbolized by the cathedral and creates an ascension of imagery from hell to "pit" to "crucifix."

In the next three stanzas the poet tells how the tower's bells are able to convey to him something of the mystery of poetic creation itself. If the tower is seen as a counterpart of the poet, the bells can be regarded as the inspired songs that must rely both on the "bell-rope" and the "tower" to be sounded forth and heard. The songs will find their release even if it means that they will "break down their tower" in so doing. In this image Crane alludes to the dynamism of poetic knowledge; poems will *out* even at the poet's expense. Thus the bells of inspiration literally rule the tower and recall not only the "long-scattered score/Of broken intervals" to the despondent poet but the sad history of "banked voices" and "terraced echoes."

> Have you not heard, have you not seen that corps
> Of shadows in the tower, whose shoulders sway
> Antiphonal carillons launched before
> The stars are caught and hived in the sun's ray?
>
> The bells, I say, the bells break down their tower;
> And swing I know not where. Their tongues engrave
> Membrane through marrow, my long-scattered score
> Of broken intervals. . . . And I, their sexton slave!
>
> Oval encyclicals in canyons heaping
> The impasse high with choir. Banked voices slain!
> Pagodas, campaniles with reveilles outleaping—
> O terraced echoes prostrate on the plain! . . .

In the next stanza, which serves as the poem's center, the poet explicitly describes his mission in the world and his inescapable need to ring out his song and to trace the "instant" voice of love that all men desperately seek. But the directness of this creed-like statement is followed by a question that receives no answer. The poet wonders if the "word" that he has "poured" and will pour from his spirit has really been his own or if it has been the "word" of the "tribunal monarch of the air" whose purpose it is to make the poet his instrument of hope only to lead him to a final despair. Although this speculation is left unresolved in the poem, the poet somehow becomes strangely reconciled to the power of poetry that threatens to undo him. This reconciliation could be prompted by the poet's realization that the "latent power" of poetry, regardless of its source, still must seek its expression in and through "sweet mortality." Whether the "word" is the poet's or that of the "tribunal monarch" is academic; it still must find its saying in the flesh of the living poet. It is in the blood of the poet, therefore, that poetry is felt and retained and purified. By continuing the struggle with the poetry that seeks its release from an "angelus of wars" that rages within him, the poet can find some promise of peace. These "wars" may eventually subdue him in the sense that the "bells break down their tower." But the poet still can know that his destruction has set free the "latent power" of the "word," and in this realization lies his victory.

The creative-destructive power of poetry that is purified in the "blood" of the poet's humanity builds the impermanent tower that is ultimately destined to be a falling down of "pebbles." This inspiration and poetic energy build the tower (poet) only to destroy it after it has served its purpose. But while it stands, the tower "unseals" the earth and, as the bells of poetry ring, "lifts love in its shower" of purified "echoes" over "the broken world."

In "The Broken Tower" Crane has succeeded in dramatizing not only the mystery of poetic creation in the style and idiom of his best poetry, but he has also succeeded in dramatizing himself and what he considered to be his mission. If the tower symbolizes the poet, it cannot help but symbolize Crane. Out of the almost insane months of his Mexican degradations Crane rallied his genius for what was to be his final "word."

If Crane in his less impressive poems seems like a man intent on satirizing himself, he is in his best poems a poet intent on transcending himself. The transcendence of "The Broken Tower" does much to refute the claim of a decline of Crane's poetic power in those final years in New York and Mixcoac and Taxco before he leaped into the sargasso fields of the Caribbean eighteen miles off the Florida keys. Out of the self-doubt and inquisition of the intricate verses of "The Broken Tower" came one verse that was a moment of self-knowledge:

> And so it was I entered the broken world
> To trace the visionary company of love, its voice
> An instant in the wind (I know not whither hurled)
> But not for long to hold each desperate choice.

7

✍ BENEATH THE MYTH

THE LIFE of Hart Crane was essentially a succession of moments of order within periods of self-destructive disorder. It can best be described as a life of extremes. The poet could exult in moments of true creative glory and, with the same sense of purpose, descend for days into drunkenness and perversion. These paradoxes in Crane's character have elicited curious responses from his admirers and detractors. To some the final artistic tragedy and triumph stemmed directly out of the poet's conflict with society. To others the poet's disordered life and incapacity to adjust to modern society were reflected in his poems and in his inability to construct and sustain his themes in an orderly fashion.

To the poet Allen Ginsberg, Crane emerges as a symbol of the martyred American artist. In a poem called "Death to Van Gogh's Ear" Ginsberg identifies the suicides of Crane and the Russian poet, Mayakovsky, as acts capable of regenerating the societies that ostracized them. When Ginsberg says that "all the governments will fall" except the "good ones" that "exist in the deaths" of Crane and Mayakovsky, he means that society is capable of being redeemed only by the blood of the poet.

Ginsberg's attitude and all those that resemble it do much to perpetuate the Crane myth. Attempting to establish contact with Whitman, Ginsberg finds in Crane not only a convenient link but the seemingly ideal symbol of a poet victimized by the dehumanizing materialism of American society. The Hart Crane of Ginsberg's poem is not so much commemorated as he is transformed.

Having interpreted the suicide as a sacrifice, Ginsberg surrounds Crane with the aura of martyrdom and would have us see him thus transfigured and thus immortalized.

But there are other critics of Crane who have written post-scripts that are as far removed from Ginsberg's memorialization as realism will permit. Peter Viereck, for instance, sees Crane as a mere perpetuator of the heedless optimism of his time. Discussing certain parallels between Crane and Vachel Lindsay, Viereck traces the undoing of both men to their failure to accept the "conservative fact that unqualified optimism about human nature results in disaster." He adds that both Lindsay and Crane were driven to self-destruction when the

> crushing of the individual in modern mechanization became too unbearable to affirm. The modern poet of progress may try to keep up his optimistic grin for his readers while the custard pie of "higher vaudeville" drips down his face. But past a certain point, he can no longer keep up the grin, whether psychologically in his private life or aesthetically in his public poetry. Our over-adjusted standardization becomes just one custard pie too many for the unadjusted poet to affirm, no matter how desperately he tries to out shout his inner tragic insight. . . . Lindsay and Crane committed suicide in 1931 and 1932 respectively, in both cases in that depression era which seemed temporarily to end the boundless optimism of American material progress.[1]

The views of Ginsberg and Viereck represent only two extremes of the varied critical attitudes towards Crane's achievement, and at what level the final estimate will come to rest cannot be predicted so easily. Doubtless, many will still look for the estimate of his literary worth in the fact of the final tragedy, the suicide, for, when a man takes his own life, it invariably encourages others to look for a reason why.

In Crane's case this has led some to conclude that suicide was a predictable dramatic end for a poet during the twenties. They contend that this was simply the culmination of the racking despair that an American poet would feel in an age whose hallmarks were corruption, bigotry, convention, idolism, intoxication, pretentiousness, idealism, and a host of other obvious terms to describe the ills and forms of society.

It would be an oversimplification, however, to say that Hart Crane was not able to prevent himself from experiencing the often

[1] "The Crack-Up of American Optimism," *Modern Age* iv–3 (Summer, 1960.)

fatal disillusionment that was one of the common legacies of his time. No poet is a mere product of his time, and Crane was no exception. It is true, however, that Crane never found a place for himself in the decade in which he did his best work and that this sense of displacement contributed to his growing feelings of despair. But the dominant pattern of Crane's life was that the heights he reached as an artist were often counterbalanced by periods of prolonged dissipation and alcoholism from which he could not extricate himself. In a very real sense he was something of a tragic hero doing battle with weaknesses he seemed unable to check. It was from his personal instabilities that, ultimately, his tragedy came.

The tragedy of Crane's life should not and, in fact, cannot obscure his poetic achievement. Nor should it blind us to the dilemmas in which many artists of the twenties found themselves. For Hart Crane dramatized so many of the problems of the American artist that it is not surprising that some of his fellow poets have eulogized him almost as if they were writing of something within themselves. Among contemporary poets there is Robert Lowell who speaks of Crane as a "stranger in America" and the "Shelley of my age." Among the poets of an earlier generation there is John Wheelwright who, in the concluding lines of his epitaph for Crane, wrote:

> What was the soil whence your anger sprang, who are deaf
> as the stones to the whispering flight of the Mississippi's rivers?
> What did you see as you fell?   What did you hear as you sank?
> Did it make you drunken with hearing?
> I will not ask any more.   You saw or heard no evil.[2]

2 "Fish Food: An Obituary to Hart Crane" from *Selected Poems* (New Directions, 1941).

135

SELECTED BIBLIOGRAPHY

POETRY, PROSE, AND CORRESPONDENCE OF HART CRANE

√ *The Collected Poems of Hart Crane.* New York: Liveright, 1933.
[This edition, now available as an Anchor paperback, contains
*The Bridge, White Buildings, Key West: An Island Sheaf, Un-
collected Poems, Early Poems,* and Crane's essay *Modern
Poetry.*]

The Letters of Hart Crane, ed. Brom Weber. New York: Hermit-
age House, 1952.

BIOGRAPHIES

Horton, Philip. *Hart Crane: The Life of an American Poet.* New
York: W. W. Norton, 1937. [This excellent biography, now
available as a Viking Compass paperback, also contains in several appendices Crane's *General Aims and Theories* and significant letters from Crane to Harriet Monroe, Otto Kahn,
and Gorham Munson.]

Weber, Brom. *Hart Crane: A Biographical and Critical Study.*
New York: The Bodley Press, 1948.

BIBLIOGRAPHY

Rowe, H. D. *Hart Crane: A Bibliography.* Denver: Alan Swallow, 1955.

CRITICAL STUDIES

Separate Work

Dembo, L. S. *Hart Crane's Sanskrit Charge: A Study of* The
Bridge. Ithaca: Cornell University Press, 1960. [This is
one of the best book-length studies of *The Bridge* to date.]

General Studies containing Chapters on Crane

Alvarez, A. *Stewards of Excellence.* New York: Scribner's, 1958.
[See "The Lyric of Hart Crane," 107–123.]

Anderson, George K., and Walton, Eda L. (eds.). *This Generation.* Chicago: Scott, Foresman, 1949.

Blackmur, Richard P. *The Double Agent.* New York: Arrow
Editions, 1935.

Blackmur, Richard P. *Form and Value in Modern Poetry.* New York: Anchor, 1946. [See "New Thresholds, New Anatomies!" 269–285.]

———. *Language as Gesture.* New York: Harcourt, Brace, 1952.

Bogan, Louise. *Achievement in American Poetry: 1900–1950.* Chicago: Henry Regnery, 1951.

Brooks, Cleanth, and Warren, Robert Penn. *Understanding Poetry.* New York: Holt, 1960. [See critique of "At Melville's Tomb," 320–323.]

Cowley, Malcolm. *Exile's Return: A Literary Odyssey of the 1920's.* New York: Viking, 1951.

———. *The Literary Situation.* New York: Viking, 1947.

Deutsch, Babette. *This Modern Poetry.* New York: W. W. Norton, 1935.

Drew, Elizabeth. *Directions in Modern Poetry.* New York: W. W. Norton, 1940.

Eastman, Max. *The Literary Mind: Its Place in an Age of Science.* New York: Scribner's, 1932.

Frank, Waldo. *In the American Jungle.* New York: Farrar and Rinehart, 1937.

Ginestier, Paul. *The Poet and the Machine.* Chapel Hill: University of North Carolina Press, 1961.

Gregory, Horace, and Zaturenska, Marya. *A History of American Poetry: 1900–1940.* New York: Harcourt, Brace, 1942.

Hoffman, Frederick. *The Twenties.* New York: Viking, 1955.

Isaacs, J. *The Background of Modern Poetry.* New York: Dutton, 1958.

Kreymborg, Alfred. *Our Singing Strength.* New York: Coward, McCann, 1929.

Kunitz, Stanley J., and Haycraft, Howard. *Twentieth Century Authors: A Biographical Dictionary of Modern Literature.* New York: H. W. Wilson, 1942.

Le Clair, Margaret F. *Lectures on Some Modern Poets.* Pittsburgh: Carnegie Institute of Technology Press, 1955. [See "Hart Crane: Poet of the Machine Age."]

Lewis, R. W. B. *The American Adam.* Chicago: University of Chicago Press, 1955.

Matthiessen, F. O. *Dictionary of American Biography* (Supplement I, Vol. 21). New York: Scribner's, 1944. [See "Crane, Harold Hart."]

Miller, James E., Jr., Shapiro, Karl, and Slote, Bernice. *Start with the Sun.* Lincoln: University of Nebraska Press, 1960. [This contains several excellent essays on Crane's aesthetic, his indebtedness to Whitman, and his rationale of *The Bridge.*]

Moore, Geoffrey (ed.). *The Penguin Book of Modern American Verse.* Baltimore: Penguin, 1954.

Munson, Gorham B. *Destinations: A Canvas of American Litera-
    ture Since 1900.* New York: J. H. Sears, 1928.
O'Connor, William Van. *Sense and Sensibility in Modern Poetry.*
    Chicago: University of Chicago Press, 1948; New York:
    Barnes & Noble, University Paperbacks, 1963.
Quinn, Sister M. Bernetta. *The Metamorphic Tradition in Mod-
    ern Poetry.* New Brunswick: Rutgers University Press, 1955.
    [Comments on Crane appear in "Eliot and Crane: *Protean
    Techniques,*" 147–167.]
Riding, Laura, and Graves, Robert. *A Survey of Modernist
    Poetry.* New York: Doubleday, Doran, 1928.
Rosenthal, M. L. *The Modern Poets.* New York: Oxford, 1960.
    [The examination of "Voyages" is particularly good.]
Rukeyser, Muriel. *The Life of Poetry.* New York: A. A. Wyn,
    1949. [See the critique of "The Broken Tower."]
Savage, D. S. *The Personal Principle: Studies in Modern Poetry.*
    London: Routledge, 1944. [See "The Americanism of Hart
    Crane," 113–120.]
Shapiro, Karl. *Poets at Work.* New York: Harcourt, Brace,
    1948. [See "The Meaning of the Discarded Poem," 83–121.]
Southworth, James G. *Some Modern American Poets.* Oxford:
    Blackwell, 1950.
Spiller, Robert E. *Cycle of American Literature.* New York:
    Macmillan, 1955.
———, et al. *Library History of the United States.* New York:
    Macmillan, 1948. [See Vol. 2, 1344–1346, and Vol. 3, 457–
    458.]
Tate, Allen. *Forlorn Demon: Didactic and Critical Essays.* Chi-
    cago: Henry Regnery, 1953.
———. *On the Limits of Poetry: Selected Essays, 1928–1948.*
    New York: Alan Swallow and William Morrow, 1948.
———. *Reactionary Essays on Poetry and Ideas.* New York:
    Scribner's, 1936.
———. *The Man of Letters in the Modern World.* New York:
    Meridian, 1955.
Unger, Leonard, and O'Connor, William Van. *Poems for Study.*
    New York: Rinehart, 1953.
Van Doren, Mark. *Introduction to Poetry.* New York: William
    Sloane Associates, 1950. [See the critique of "Praise for an
    Urn," 102–107.]
Viereck, Peter. *Strike through the Mask.* New York: Scribner's,
    1950. [This contains an analysis of machine symbolism in
    "The Poet of the Machine Age."]
Waggoner, Hyatt Howe. *The Heel of Elohim: Science and Values
    in Modern Poetry.* Norman: University of Oklahoma Press,
    1950.

Wells, Henry W. *The American Way of Poetry.* New York: Columbia University Press, 1943.

Wilder, Amos N. *The Spiritual Aspects of the New Poetry.* New York: Harper's, 1940.

Wilson, Edmund. *The Shores of Light: A Literary Chronicle of the Twenties and Thirties.* New York: Farrar, Strauss and Young, 1952.

Winters, Yvor. *In Defense of Reason.* New York: Alan Swallow and William Morrow, 1947.

————. *On Modern Poets.* New York: Meridian, 1959.

————. *Primitivism and Decadence: A Study of American Experimental Poetry.* New York: Arrow Editions, 1937.

Critical Articles

Aiken, Conrad. "Hart Crane," *The Atlantic Monthly,* CLX (August, 1937), vi.

Allen, Charles. "The Advance Guard," *Sewanee Review,* II (Summer, 1943), 410–429.

Atkins, Elizabeth. "Man and Animals in Recent Poetry," *PMLA,* LI (March, 1936), 263–283. [Critique of Crane's "A Name for All."]

Baird, Peggy. "The Last Days of Hart Crane," *Venture,* IV–1 (1961).

Beach, Joseph Warren. "The Cancelling Out—A Note on Recent Poetry," *Accent,* VII (Summer, 1947). [*The Bridge* is treated.]

Benét, William Rose. "Round about Parnassus," *Saturday Review of Literature,* VI (July 5, 1930), 1176. [Review of *The Bridge.*]

Bewley, Marius. "Hart Crane's Last Poem," *Accent,* XIX–2 (Spring, 1959), 75–85.

Blake, Howard. "Thoughts on Modern Poetry," *Sewanee Review,* XLII (April–June, 1935), 187–196.

Calmer, Alan. "The Case of Hart Crane," *New Republic,* LXXI (July 20, 1932), 264.

Coffman, Stanley K., Jr. "Symbolism in *The Bridge,*" *PMLA,* LXV (March, 1951), 65–77.

Cowley, Malcolm. "The Leopard in Hart Crane's Brow," *Esquire,* L (October, 1958), 257–258, 260, 264, 266, 268, 270–271.

Davison, E. "The Symbol and the Poets," *Yale Review,* XXXII (Autumn 1933), 178–182. [A critique of *The Bridge.*]

Dembo L. S. "Hart Crane's Early Poetry," *University of Kansas City Review,* XXVII–3 (March, 1961), 181–187.

"Discussion with Hart Crane," *Poetry: A Magazine of Verse,* XXIX (October, 1926), 34–41.

Drew, Elizabeth. "The Trouble with Modern Poetry," *Saturday*

Review of Literature, XIV (May 23, 1936), 3–4, 14. [Critique of *The Bridge*.]

Frank, Joseph. "Hart Crane: American Poet," *Sewanee Review*, LXII (Winter, 1949). [A review of Weber's study of Crane.]

Frank, Waldo. "The Poetry of Hart Crane," *New Republic*, L (March 16, 1927), 116–117.

———. "Introduction to Hart Crane," *New Republic*, LXXIV (February 15, 1933), 11–16.

Friedman, Paul. "*The Bridge*: A Study in Symbolism," *Psychoanalytic Quarterly*, XXI (January, 1952), 49–80. [A study of sexual symbolism in *The Bridge*.]

Ghiselin, Brewster. "Bridge into the Sea," *Partisan Review*, XVI (July, 1949), 679–686.

Gregory, Horace. "American Poetry: 1930–1940," *Accent*, I (Summer, 1941), 213–228.

Herman, Barbara. "The Language of Hart Crane," *Sewanee Review*, LXIII (Winter, 1950), 52–67.

Hoffman, Frederick J. "The Technological Fallacy in Contemporary Poetry: Hart Crane and McKnight Black," *American Literature*, XXI (March, 1949), 94–107.

Honig, Edward. "American Poetry and the Rationalist Critic," *Virginia Quarterly*, XXXVI–3 (Summer, 1960), 416–429.

Juniper, Will C. "Crane's 'For the Marriage of Faustus and Helen,'" *Explicator*, XVII (Item 8).

Larrabee, Ankey. "The Symbol of the Sea in Crane's 'Voyages,'" *Accent*, III (Winter, 1943).

McLaughlin, John. "Imagemes and Allo-Images in a poem by Hart Crane," *Folio*, XXIII–2 (Spring, 1958), 48–64. [A critique of "Lachrymae Christi."]

Martey, Herbert. "Hart Crane's 'The Broken Tower': A Study in Technique," *University of Kansas City Review*, XVIII (Spring, 1952), 199–205.

Matthiessen, F. O. "American Poetry, 1920–1940," *Sewanee Review*, LV (January–March, 1947), 24–55.

Miles, Josephine. "The Poetry of Praise," *Kenyon Review*, XXIII–1 (Winter, 1961), 104–125.

Moss, Howard. "Disorder as Myth: Hart Crane's *The Bridge*," *Poetry: A Magazine of Verse*, LXII (April, 1943), 32–45.

O'Connor, William Van. "The Influence of the Metaphysicals on Modern Poetry," *College English*, IX (January, 1948), 180–187.

Pierce, Frederick E. "Four Poets," *Yale Review*, XVII (October, 1927), 176–178.

"Preface to Hart Crane," *New Republic*, LVII (April 23, 1930), 276–277.

Richman, Sidney. "Hart Crane's 'Voyages II': An Experiment in

Redemption," *Wisconsin Studies in Contemporary Literature,* III-2 (Spring–Summer, 1962), 65–78.

Shockley, Martin S. "Hart Crane's 'Lachrymae Christi,'" *University of Kansas City Review,* XVI (Autumn, 1947), 31–36.

Slote, Bernice. "The Structure of Hart Crane's *The Bridge*," *University of Kansas City Review,* XXIV-3 (March, 1958), 225–238.

Swallow, Alan. "Hart Crane," *University of Kansas City Review,* XVI (Winter, 1949), 103–118.

Tate, Allen. "A Distinguished Poet," *The Hound and Horn,* III (July–September, 1930), 580–585.

Unterecker, John. "The Architecture of *The Bridge*," *Wisconsin Studies in Contemporary Literature,* III-2 (Spring–Summer, 1962), 5–20.

Viereck, Peter. "The Crack-Up of American Optimism: Vachel Lindsay, the Dante of the Fundamentalists," *Modern Age,* IV-3 (Summer, 1960), 269–284.

Waggoner, Hyatt Howe. "Hart Crane and the Broken Parabola," *University of Kansas City Review,* II (Spring, 1945), 173–177.

———. "Hart Crane's Bridge to Cathay," *American Literature,* XVI (May, 1944), 115–130.

Walcutt, Charles C. "Voyages," *Explicator,* IV (June, 1946), 53.

Winters, Yvor. "The Progress of Hart Crane," *Poetry: A Magazine of Verse,* XXXVI (June, 1930), 153–165. [A review of *The Bridge.*]

UPDATED BIBLIOGRAPHY

BIOGRAPHY

Unterecker, John E. *Voyager: A Life of Hart Crane*. New York: Farrar, Straus & Giroux, 1969.

BIBLIOGRAPHICAL STUDIES

Bloomingdale, Judith. "Three Decades in Periodical Criticism of Hart Crane's *The Bridge*," *Papers of the Bibliographical Society of America*, LVII (July-September 1963), 364-371.

Katz, Joseph. "CALM Addendum No. 1: Hart Crane," *Papers of the Bibliographical Society of America*, LXIII (2nd Quarter, 1969), 130.

Keller, Dean H. "CALM Addenda No. 2: Hart Crane," *Papers of the Bibliographical Society of America*, LXIV (1st Quarter, 1970), 98-99.

Lane, Gary, ed. *A Concordance to the Poems of Hart Crane*. New York: Haskell House, 1972.

Lohf, Kenneth A. "The Library of Hart Crane," *Proof*, III (1973), 283-334.

———. *The Literary Manuscripts of Hart Crane*. Columbus: Ohio State University Press, 1967.

———. "The Prose Manuscripts of Hart Crane: An Editorial Portfolio," *Proof*, II (1972), 1-60.

Schwartz, Joseph. *Hart Crane: An Annotated Critical Bibliography*. New York: David Lewis, 1970.

Schwartz, Joseph, and Robert C. Schweik. *Hart Crane: A Descriptive Bibliography*. Pittsburgh: University of Pittsburgh Press, 1972.

———. "CALM Addendum No. 3: The Literary Manuscripts of Hart Crane," *Papers of the Bibliographical Society of America*, LXVI (1st Quarter, 1972), 64-65.

Simon, Marc. "CALM Addendum No. 4: Hart Crane," *Papers of the Bibliographical Society of America*, LXVIII (1st Quarter, 1974), 69.

Weber, Brom. "Hart Crane," in *Sixteen Modern Authors: A Survey of Research and Criticism*, ed. Jackson R. Bryer. Durham, N. C.: Duke University Press, 1974.

White, William. "Hart Crane: Bibliographical Addenda," *Bulletin of Bibliography*, XXIV (September-December 1963), 35.

SEPARATE WORKS

Butterfield, R. W. *The Broken Arc: A Study of Hart Crane.* Edinburgh: Oliver & Boyd, 1969.

Leibowitz, Herbert A. *Hart Crane: An Introduction to the Poetry.* New York: Columbia University Press, 1968.

Lewis, R. W. B. *The Poetry of Hart Crane: A Critical Study.* Princeton, N. J.: Princeton University Press, 1967.

Perry, Robert L. *The Shared Vision of Waldo Frank and Hart Crane.* Lincoln: University of Nebraska, 1966.

Quinn, Vincent. *Hart Crane.* New York: Twayne, 1963.

Paul, Sherman. *Hart's Bridge.* Urbana: University of Illinois Press, 1972.

Spears, Monroe K. *Hart Crane.* Minneapolis: University of Minnesota Press, 1965.

Uroff, M. D. *Hart Crane: The Patterns of His Poetry.* Urbana: University of Illinois Press, 1974.

Voelcker, Hunce. *The Hart Crane Voyages.* New York: Brownstone Press, 1967.

GENERAL STUDIES CONTAINING CHAPTERS ON CRANE

Andreach, Robert J. *Studies in Structure.* New York: Fordham University Press, 1964.

Beach, Joseph Warren. *Obsessive Images,* ed. William Van O'Connor. Minneapolis: University of Minnesota Press, 1966.

Cambon, Glauco. *The Inclusive Flame.* Bloomington: Indiana University Press, 1963.

Clark, David R. *Lyric Resonance.* Amherst: University of Massachusetts Press, 1972.

Dembo, L. S. *Conceptions of Reality in Modern American Poetry.* Berkley and Los Angeles: University of California Press, 1966.

Fowlie, Wallace. *Love in Literature: Studies in Symbolic Expression.* Bloomington: Indiana University Press, 1965.

Fussell, Edwin. *Lucifer in Harness: American Meter, Metaphor, and Diction.* Princeton, N. J.: Princeton University Press, 1973.

Gross, Harvey. *Sound and Form in Modern Poetry.* Ann Arbor: University of Michigan Press, 1965.

Jennings, Elizabeth. *Every Changing Shape.* London: Andre Deutsch, 1961.

Landry, Hilton. "Of Prayer and Praise: The Poetry of Hart Crane," in *The Twenties: Poetry and Prose,* ed. Richard E. Langford and William E. Taylor. Deland, Fla.: Everett/Edwards, 1966.

Lutyens, David Bulwer. *The Creative Encounter.* London: Secker & Warburg, 1960.

Morgan, H. Wayne. *Writers in Transition: Seven Americans.* New York: Hill & Wang, 1963.

Nassar, Eugene Paul. *The Rape of Cinderella.* Bloomington: Indiana University Press, 1970.

Pearce, Roy Harvey. *The Continuity of American Poetry.* Princeton, N. J.: Princeton University Press, 1961.

Riddell, Joseph N. "Hart Crane's Poetics of Failure," in *Modern American Poetry: Essays in Criticism,* ed. Jerome Mazzaro. New York: David McKay, 1970.

Trachtenberg, Allan. *Brooklyn Bridge: Fact and Symbol.* New York: Oxford University Press, 1965.

Van Nostrand, Albert. "*The Bridge* and Hart Crane's 'Span of Consciousness,' " in *Aspects of American Poetry,* ed. R. M. Ludwig. Columbus: Ohio State University Press, 1962.

―――. *Everyman His Own Poet: Romantic Gospels in American Literature.* New York: McGraw-Hill, 1968.

Vogler, Thomas A. *Preludes to Vision: The Epic Venture in Blake, Wordsworth, Keats, and Hart Crane.* Berkley and Los Angeles: University of California Press, 1971.

Waggoner, Hyatt A. *American Poets: From the Puritans to the Present.* Boston: Houghton Mifflin, 1968.

CRITICAL ARTICLES

Anderson, David D. "Journey Through Time: The Poetic Vision of Hart Crane," *Ohioana Quarterly,* XV (Summer 1972), 59-64.

Arpad, Joseph J. "Hart Crane's Platonic Myth: The Brooklyn Bridge," *American Literature,* XXXIX (March 1967), 75-86.

Baker, John. "Commercial Sources for Hart Crane's *The River,*" *Wisconsin Studies in Contemporary Literature,* VI (Winter-Spring 1965), 45-55.

Bartra, Augusti. "New York: Two Poetic Impressions," *Americas,* XVIII (October 1966), 14-22.

Bassoff, Bruce. "Crane's 'For the Marriage of Faustus and Helen,' iii, 1-23," *Explicator,* XXXI (March 1973), item 53.

―――. "Rhetorical Pressures in 'For the Marriage of Faustus and Helen," *Concerning Poetry,* V (Fall 1972), 40-48.

Braun, Henry. "Hart Crane's 'The Broken Tower,' " *Boston University Studies, in English,* V (Autumn 1961), 167-177.

Brown, Susan Jenkins. "Hart Crane: The End of the Harvest: Hart Crane's Letters to William Slater Brown and Susan Jenkins Brown," *The Southern Review,* IV (Autumn 1968), 945-1014.

Brunner, Edward. "'Your Hands Within My Hands Are Deeds': Poems of Love in *The Bridge*," *Iowa Review*, IV (Winter 1973), 105-126.

Bryant, J. A., Jr. "Hart Crane and the Illusory Abyss," *The Sewanee Review*, LXXVII (Winter 1969), 149-154.

Clark, David R. "Hart Crane's Technique," *Texas Studies in Language and Literature*, V (Autumn 1963), 389-397.

Davison, R. A. "Hart Crane, Louis Untermeyer, and T. S. Eliot: A New Crane Letter," *American Literature*, XLIV (March 1972), 143-146.

Day, Robert A. "Image and Idea in Voyages II," *Criticism*, VII (Summer 1965), 224-234.

Dembo, L. S. "Hart Crane's Verticalist Poem," *American Literature*, XL (March 1968), 77-81.

Dickinson-Brown, Roger. "Crane's 'For the Marriage of Faustus and Helen,' ii, 7-8 and 11-12," *Explicator*, XXXI (April 1973), item 66.

Friedman, Judith S., and Ruth Perlmutter. "Crane's 'Voyages II,'" *Explicator*, XIX (October 1960), item 4.

Griffith, Ben W., Jr. "Crane's 'Paraphrase,'" *Explicator*, XIII (October 1954), item 5.

Grigsby, Gordon K. "Hart Crane's Doubtful Vision," *College English*, XXIV (April 1963), 518-523.

———. "The Photographs in the First Edition of *The Bridge*," *Texas Studies in Language and Literature*, IV (Spring 1962), 5-11.

Guillory, Daniel. "Hart Crane, Marianne Moore, and the Brooklyn Bridge," *Ball State University Forum*, XV (Summer 1974), 48-49.

Gulpin, Alfred. "A Boat in the Tower: Rimbaud in Cleveland, 1922," *Renascence*, XXV (Autumn 1972), 3-13.

Hinz, Evelyn J. "Hart Crane's 'Voyages' Reconsidered," *Contemporary Literature*, XIII (Summer 1972), 315-333.

Holton, Milne. "'A Baudelairesque Thing': The Directions of Hart Crane's 'Black Tambourine,'" *Criticism*, IX (Summer 1967), 215-228.

Irwin, John T. "Naming Names: Hart Crane's 'Logic of Metaphor,'" *The Southern Review*, XI (April 1975), 284-299.

Kahn, Sy. "Hart Crane and Harry Crosby: A Transity of Poets," *Journal of Modern Literature*, I (1970), 45-56.

Kessler, Edward. "Crane's 'Black Tambourine,'" *Explicator*, XXIX (September 1971), item 4.

Kloucek, Jerome W. "The Framework of Hart Crane's *The Bridge*," *Midwest Review*, II (Spring 1960), 13-34.

Knox, George. "Crane and Sulla: Conjunction of Painterly and Poetic Worlds," *Texas Studies in Language and Literature*, XII (Winter 1971), 689-707.

———. " 'Sight, Sound and Flesh': Synoptic View from Crane's Tower," *Markham Review*, III (October 1971), 1-10.

Koretz, Jean, Virginia Mosely, and John R. Willingham, "Crane's 'Passage,' " *Explicator*, XIII (June 1955), item 47.

Kramer, Maurice. "Hart Crane's 'Reflexes,' " *Twentieth Century Literature*, XIII (October 1967), 131-138.

———. "Six Voyages of a Derelict Seer," *The Sewanee Review*, LXXIII (July-September 1965), 410-423.

Kramer, Victor. "The 'Mid-Kingdom' of Crane's 'Black Tambourine' and Toomer's *Cane*," *CLA Journal*, XVII (June 1974), 486-497.

La France, Marston. "The Bridge-Builder," *Canadian Review of American Studies*, II (Fall 1972), 106-113.

Leggett, Bernie. "Crane's 'The Mango Tree,' " *Explicator*, XXXII (November 1973), item 18.

Lewis, R. W. B. "Crane's Visionary Lyric: The Way to the Bridge," *The Massachusetts Review*, VII (Spring 1966), 227-253.

———. "Hart Crane and the Clown Tradition," *The Massachusetts Review*, IV (Summer 1963), 745-767.

Lyon, Melvin E. "Crane's 'The Mango Tree,' " *Explicator*, XXV (1967), item 48.

McClintock, Patricia. "A Reading of Hart Crane's 'For the Marriage of Faustus and Helen," *Massachusetts Studies in English*, I (1967), 39-43.

McMichael, James. "Hart Crane," *The Southern Review*, VIII (April 1972), 290-309.

Metzger, Deena Posy. "Hart Crane's *Bridge*: The Myth Active," *The Arizona Quarterly*, XX (Spring 1964), 36-46.

Paniker, Kayyappa. "Myth and Machine in Hart Crane," *Literary Criterion*, IX (Summer 1971), 27-41.

Parkinson, Thomas. "The Hart Crane-Yvor Winters Correspondence," *The Ohio Review*, XVI (Fall 1974), 5-24.

Perry, Robert L. "Critical Problems in Hart Crane's 'Chaplinesque,' " *Concerning Poetry*, VIII (Fall 1975), 23-27.

Porter, Frank. " 'Chaplineque': An Explication," *English Journal*, LVII (February 1968), 191-192.

Poulin, A., Jr. "Crane's 'Voyages II,' " *Explicator*, XXVIII (1970), item 15.

Riddel, Joseph. "Hart Crane's Poetics of Failure," *Journal of English Literary History*, XXXIII (1966), 473-496.

Runden, John P. "Whitman's *The Sleepers* and the 'Indiana' section of Crane's *The Bridge*," *Walt Whitman Review*, XV (December 1969), 245-248.

Rupp, Richard H. "Hart Crane: Vitality as *Credo* in 'Atlantis,' " *The Midwest Quarterly*, III (1962), 265-275.

Sanders, Thomas E. "Crane's 'The Return,'" *Explicator*, X (December 1951), item 20.

Scannell, Vernon. "The Ecstatic Muse: Some Notes on Hart Crane," *The Contemporary Review*, CXCIX (May 1961), 231-237.

Scarlett, John R. "Crane's 'The Sad Indian,'" *Explicator*, XXIX (1971), item 69.

Schulz, Max F. "Crane's 'Voyages' 1-5, 21-25," *Explicator*, XIV (April 1956), item 46.

Sheehan, Peter J. "Crane's 'Moment Fugue,'" *Explicator*, XXXI (May 1973), item 78.

———. "Hart Crane and the Contemporary Search," *English Journal*, LX (December 1971), 1209-1213.

Simon, Marc. "Hart Crane and Samuel B. Greenberg: An Emblematic Interlude," *Contemporary Literature*, XII (Spring 1971), 166-172.

Simpson, William T. "An Explication of Hart Crane's 'Black Tambourine,'" *Xavier University Studies*, VII (1967), 5-7.

Slate, Joseph Evand. "William Carlos Williams, Hart Crane, and 'The Virtue of History,'" *Texas Studies in Language and Literature*, VI (1965), 486-511.

Sugg, Richard P. "The Imagination's White Buildings and 'Quaker Hill,'" *Erasmus Review*, I (1971), 145-155.

Unterecker, John E. "A Piece of Pure Invention," *Forum*, V (1967), 42-44.

Widmer, Kinsley. "Crane's 'Key West,'" *Explicator*, XVIII (December 1959), item 17.

Yanella, P. R. "Inventive Dust: The Metamorphoses of Faustus and Helen," *Contemporary Literature*, XV (Winter 1974), 102-122.

———. "Toward Apotheosis: Hart Crane's Visionary Lyrics," *Criticism*, X (Fall 1968), 313-333.

Young, James Dean. "Hart Crane's 'Repose of Rivers': What's the Evidence? A System for Critics," *Xavier University Studies*, II (1963), 121-137.

Zigerell, James. "Crane's 'Voyages II,'" *Explicator*, XIII (November 1954), item 7.

INDEX

Index

Index